THE WILDERNESS

Also by Maurya Simon

The Enchanted Room (Copper Canyon Press, 1986)

Days of Awe (Copper Canyon Press, 1989)

Speaking in Tongues (Gibbs Smith Publishers, 1990)

The Golden Labyrinth (University of Missouri Press, 1995)

A Brief History of Punctuation (Sutton Hoo Press, 2002)

Ghost Orchid (Red Hen Press, 2004)

WEAVERS (Blackbird Press, 2005)

Cartographies: Uncollected Poems: 1980–2005 (Red Hen Press, 2008)

The Raindrop's Gospel: The Trials of St. Jerome and St. Paula (Elixir Press, 2010)

Questions My Daughters Asked Me, Answers I Never Gave Them (Blackbird Press, 2014)

THE WILDERNESS

New & Selected Poems

1980–2016

MAURYA SIMON

Red Hen Press | *Pasadena, CA*

Cover image: Copyright © 2018 by Baila Goldenthal, No. 12 in *Weavers Series* (1992)
Book design: Madi R. Foster & Hannah Moye

Library of Congress Cataloging-in-Publication Data
Name: Simon, Maurya, 1950–author.
Title: The wilderness: new and selected poems / Maurya Simon.
Description: Pasadena, California: Red Hen Press, [2018]
Identifiers: LCCN 2017052116 | ISBN 9781597096102 (casebound) |
    ISBN 9781597092494 (softcover) | ISBN 9781597097581 (ebook)
Classification: LCC PS3569.I4827 A6 2018 | DDC 811/.54—dc23
LC record available at https://lccn.loc.gov/2017052116

The National Endowment for the Arts, the Los Angeles County Arts Commission, the Ah-
manson Foundation, the Dwight Stuart Youth Fund, the Max Factor Family Foundation,
the Pasadena Tournament of Roses Foundation, the Pasadena Arts & Culture Commission
and the City of Pasadena Cultural Affairs Division, the City of Los Angeles Department of
Cultural Affairs, the Audrey & Sydney Irmas Charitable Foundation, the Kinder Morgan
Foundation, the Allergan Foundation, the Riordan Foundation, and the Amazon Literary
Partnership partially support Red Hen Press.

First Edition
Published by Red Hen Press
www.redhen.org

Acknowledgments

I wish to acknowledge and thank the editors of the following literary journals, presses, and poetry anthologies in which these poems, chapbooks, broadsides, and volumes originally appeared:

Questions My Daughters Asked Me, Answers I Never Gave Them (Blackbird Press, 2014): My gratitude to Jean Gillingwators, editor and publisher of Blackbird Press, and to her assistant, Anna Aquitela, for producing this beautiful letterpress book.

The Enchanted Room (Copper Canyon Press, 1986): *CutBank*: "Madras Insomnia"; *The Reaper*: "Tat Tvam Asi" and "Epitaph"; *The Ear*: "The Soldier"; *Grand Street*: "The Sibyl"; *Grove Magazine*: "The Origin of Death."

Days of Awe (Copper Canyon Press, 1989): *Poetry*: "Theme and Variations"; *Cumberland Poetry Review*: "Contusion" and "King Midas's Daughter"; *The Seattle Review*: "For Naomi"; *The Southern Review*: "Breakwater"; *Areté*: "Clothes That Wear Me"; *West Branch*: "Survival"; *The Hudson Review*: "Boy Crazy"; *Poetry East*: "Madras Lament" and "Dream Babies."

Speaking in Tongues (Gibbs Smith, 1990): *The Gettysburg Review*: "Origins." This book was awarded the 1989-1990 Peregrine Smith Poetry Award. Christopher Merrill, to whom I'm deeply grateful, selected it for recognition and publication.

The Golden Labyrinth (University of Missouri Press, 1995): *Innisfree*: "The Ugly Dog" and "Karma"; *The Georgia Review*: "The Banded Krait."

A Brief History of Punctuation (Sutton Hoo Press, 2002): published first as a chapbook by *The Georgia Review* and the University of Georgia Press, 2000; later published as a limited edition, letterpress book by Sutton Hoo Press, 2002.

Ghost Orchid (Red Hen Press, 2004): *The Gettysburg Review*: "The Ravens"; *Runes* 2002: "An Unkempt Brilliance I Fear but Cannot Name"; *Mosaic*: "Unfinished Psalm"; *AGNI*: "All Souls' Day"; *American Literary Review*: "The Search"; *Poetry International*: "The Fallen Angel"; *Shirim*: "The Rapture," and reprinted as a limited edition broadside by Sutton Hoo Press, 1998; *Quarterly West*: "Black Haloes"; *The Sow's Ear Poetry Review*: "Angels," and reprinted in *Good Poems for Hard Times* (W. W. Norton & Penguin Books, 2005); *The Watershed Anthology II* (Sutton Hoo Press, 2000): "Benediction." "Benediction" also appeared on the January 2000 PoetryNet website.

WEAVERS (Blackbird Press, 2005): *The Gettysburg Review*: "Rapture." Profound thanks to Jean Gillingwators and Anna Aquitela, who both labored for nearly a decade to produce this exquisite letterpress book.

Cartographies, Uncollected Poems: 1980–2005 (Red Hen Press, 2008): *CALYX Journal*: "Snow" and reprinted in *A Fierce Brightness: Twenty-five Years of Women's Poetry* (Calyx Books, 2002); *The Gettysburg Review*: "Purview"; *American Literary Review*: "The Voyage"; *The Journal*: "Second Born"; *Spoon River Poetry Review*: "Bark with Authority"; *Pacific Review*: "Marriage Vow"; *The Kenyon Review*: "Black Widow"; *The Los Angeles Times Sunday Book Review*: "Dulce et Decorum Est"; *Mississippi Valley Review*: "City of Angels"; *Poetry East*: "El Día de los Muertos" and "Waste Management"; *Three Genres*, 8th Edition (Prentice Hall, 2006): "The Dolphin." "El Día de los Muertos" was awarded the Celia B. Wagner Award from the Poetry Society of America.

The Raindrop's Gospel: The Trials of St. Jerome and St. Paula (Elixir Press, 2010): *Prairie Schooner*: "St. Paula among the Marigolds," "St. Jerome's Lost Diaries," "A Letter from Abbess Paula the Younger"; *Poetry*: "St. Jerome in Decline"; *Smartish Pace*: "A Matriarch of Rome," "St. Jerome Rests from His Labors"; *Ploughshares*: "Father of Punctuation"; *The Journal*: "Obiter Dictum"; *New England Review*: "Paula's Tale: Mourning"; *The Southern Review*: "Hieronymus and the Lion"; *Agenda*: "St. Jerome Alone."

New Poems (2010–2016): *Kestrel, Tenth Anniversary Anthology*: "River Lamps"; *Open Doors: An Invitation to Poetry* (California State University, Fullerton): "Dawn over the Tiber River"; *The Gettysburg Review*: "Late November Lament."

I'm grateful to my fine students from the University of California, Riverside, who, for over twenty-five years, taught me to see my own work more clearly. My lasting gratitude to my sisters in letters, Cynthia Tuell, Frances McConnel, Nancy Ware, and, especially, W.J. Herbert and Peggy Shumaker, for their astute literary guidance, friendship, and aesthetic support. My sincere thanks to my husband's cousin, Morgan Brenner, and to Ryan Maganini and Michael Diaz, for their valuable technical assistance. Muchas gracias to my generous poetry mentors: the late David Van Wagoner, Richard Tillinghast, Bert Meyers, Barry Sanders, Robert Mezey, and Charles Wright. This book partly owes its final structure, its thematic trajectory, and its coherence to my brilliant colleague, the poet Elizabeth Faith Aamot: cosmic gratitude. Finally, I thank my husband, Robert Falk, for his Sanskrit translations, his wisdom, and his enduring love.

Contents

On the Poems of Maurya Simon 15
Questions My Daughters Asked Me,
    Answers I Never Gave Them 19

FROM *The Enchanted Room*

The Sibyl 25
The Origin of Death 27
The Soldier 28
Tooth Fairy 30
Snails 32
Tat Tvam Asi 33
The Bearer's Son 35
Firewalking 37
Madras Insomnia 39
Epitaph 40

FROM *Days of Awe*

Clothes That Wear Me 43
Breakwater 47
Boy Crazy 49
Dream Babies 51
For Naomi 52
Contusion 53
Theme and Variations 55
Survival 56
King Midas's Daughter 57
Madras Lament 58

FROM *Speaking in Tongues*

Origins. 63

FROM *The Golden Labyrinth*

Want 81
Dharma 82
Karma 85
Leah in the Vale of Tears 86
The Ugly Dog 87
Alex in Hindustan 90
Banded Krait 92
Elegy in a Snowstorm 94
Meditation at Twilight. 98
Bangalore Lullaby 99

FROM *A Brief History of Punctuation*

I. The Creation of the Question Mark 103
II. Ellipses 104
III. The Inception of the Colon 106
IV. The Era of the Period 108
V. The Invention of the Comma. 109
VI. Parentheses: A Bestiary. 111
VII. A Hyphenated Rondo 113
VIII. The Birth of Dashes 114
IX. Claiming the Apostrophe. 117
X. The Semicolon: A Totem 118

FROM *Ghost Orchid*

The Ravens. 121
The Search 123
The Fallen Angel 125
The Rapture 126
Black Haloes 127
All Souls' Day 129
Angels 130
Unfinished Psalm. 132
An Unkempt Brilliance I Fear but Cannot Name. 133
Transubstantiation 137
Benediction 139

FROM *WEAVERS*

I. Sisters 143
II. The Wedding Dress. 145
III. Rapture 147
IV. Madrigal. 149
V. The Virgin and the Widow. 152
VI. The House of Women 154
VII. The Healer. 157
VIII. The Saint 159
IX. Epiphany 162
X. The Unfolding 165
XI. The Dreamer 168
XII. The Magician 170
XIII. The Outcast. 173
XIV. The Lover 176
XV. Benediction 178

FROM *Cartographies*

Snow 183
Second Born 187
Purview 188
Dulce et Decorum Est 190
City of Angels 192
Bark with Authority 194
El Día de los Muertos 196
The Dolphin 198
Waste Management 199
A Small Elegy for a Big Dog 200
Marriage Vow 201
Black Widow 202
The Voyage 203
Ten Versions of Ruin and Repair 204

FROM *The Raindrop's Gospel: The Trials
    of St. Jerome and St. Paula*

Genealogies 211
Chronologies of the Lives of St. Jerome and St. Paula 212
Father of Punctuation 217
A Matriarch of Rome 219
Paula's Tale: Mourning 221
Hieronymus and the Lion 224
Obiter Dictum 226
St. Paula among the Marigolds 228
Deo Gratias 229
The Lost Diaries 231
St. Jerome in the Chalcis Desert 234
Caput Mundi 235

St. Jerome Rests from His Labors 237

St. Jerome in Decline. 239

St. Jerome Alone 242

A Letter from the Abbess Paula the Younger 244

New Poems (2010–2016)

River Lamps 249

The Women of Juárez 250

The Prisoner 251

This Lion 252

Egypt Liberated 254

I Won't Pretend 255

If I Could 256

Baila-Ma 257

Gone 259

Mother My Ship 260

Martin Falk's Last Photographs .261

The Inheritance 263

Dear Old Dad 264

The Father of All Things 266

Elegy at Midnight 267

The Consolations of Love 269

Dog Sleeping 270

Late November Lament 271

Dawn over the Tiber River 272

Notes and Dedications 275

For my husband, Robert Falk—

For my daughters, Naomi and Leah Falk—

For my grandsons, Alex Flores-Falk and Ethan Diaz—

For my granddaughter, Laila Bay Falk, newest orchid in our midst—

Long may you thrive in the wilderness

On the Poems of Maurya Simon

Introducing the poems that a poet has selected from her life's work might normally invite an examination of their evolution from early to late, although I think the real strength and uniqueness of Maurya Simon's work can best be approached through her fifth book, *A Brief History of Punctuation*. There in abundance is Simon's singular talent for seeing the world double, in metaphor and music. Ezra Pound said that the poetics of melopoeia, poetry severed from music, atrophies. Simon's richly textured, sensuous, dense lines quite save her from this mostly postmodern malady, and so she stands apart from other poets of her generation who eschewed linguistic music for the "natural" tonalities of ordinary, spoken English; and I might add here that if there is anything in poetry that is an indication of pure talent, something that cannot be taught, rather like perfect pitch in music, it is an ear for the inner life of the line, the phonemic harmonies that some linguists like to analyze in terms of phonetic symbolism but that certain poets (Dylan Thomas comes quickly to mind) know intuitively. Simon's style is a fluid, varied, high style that occasionally embraces the colloquial and quotidian while more frequently achieving an almost baroque elegance reminiscent of some of the post–WWII poets such as Wilbur, Clampitt, and Hecht.

But what is Simon's subject? To what does she give "a local habitation and a name?" In a foreward to the poems of Joseph Brodsky, W. H. Auden said that Brodsky was "a traditionalist in the sense that he is interested in what most lyric poets in all ages have been interested in, that is, in personal encounters with nature, human artifacts, persons loved or revered, and in reflections upon the human condition, death, and the meaning of existence." Like Brodsky, Simon has pursued these themes energetically, as her wonderfully moving poem, "Questions My Daughters Asked Me, Answers I Never Gave Them," which opens *The Wilderness*, tells us. Offering equally compelling testimony to her dedication and brilliant handling of the great themes is *The Golden Labyrinth*, her fourth book. This is done in the context of India, where Simon resided during her Fulbright year, where context means mortality not as the subject of some freakish epiphany but as the daily climate of the streets, and suffering not as the occasional suburban tragedy but as the bitter air that fills those streets. In her "encounters with nature," Simon (who lives high on Mt. Baldy in the Angeles National Forest) is at her best, unusually articulate and informed, a student of the natural world (an entomology major at Berkeley) with a deep understanding of the processes ("the whole heaving universe // endlessly dancing") rather than simply the names of flora and fauna as described objects.

My favorite book of Simon's, *Ghost Orchid*, known to its many fans as her "God book," seemed to me when I first read it as not only the breaking of new ground for her in terms of subject matter but a stylistic advancement (or perfection) as well, studded with lines so rich and memorable that one is compelled to read them aloud:

> Rubied maple leaves bloody the ground
>
> with tattered clues to the afterlife;
> acorns concern themselves, like plump nuns,
>
> with the sacraments of summer that worms
> sequester as holy grails. I have lost my way.

Blakean in its powers of illumination and insight, *Ghost Orchid* is a grace-haunted translation of the hieroglyphic heart, a visionary marriage of heaven and hell consummated somewhere near the crossroads of the spiritual and erotic. We encounter not only God, "who loves us all to death," but also the albino angel, "a helium virgin, / Who lifted off into space like a chrome rocket," and Beelzebub, "poet laureate of latrines" and "kingpin of sinners." In *Ghost Orchid* Simon performs poetry's ultimate task: the alchemy of body and soul.

Cartographies, Simon's most recent book of lyric poems, continues what is actually a motif that surfaces from time to time throughout her career: maps both literal and metaphorical, but especially the latter, guidebooks to the otherwise hidden inroads of the human heart. And I am thrilled that she placed what I believe to be her magnum opus at the close of *The Wilderness*, for that's what *The Raindrop's Gospel* most certainly is, offering an ingenious reconstruction of the love story of St. Jerome and St. Paula. Human in their saintliness, agonizingly saintly in their humanness, Jerome and Paula emerge in this beautifully crafted verse novel as fully realized erotic, spiritual, and intellectual beings, all the more passionate for their struggles against passion. For many poets the long poem (like the mythical Great American Novel), rather than showcasing their lyric powers, only dilutes them. Having written a few long narrative poems myself, I concluded that the only way to tackle such a beast was to make it a lyric poem at the same time. And *The Raindrop's Gospel* does this superbly.

When readers eager, or perhaps just curious, to enter the exotic, marvelous, undiscovered country of poetry for the first time nonetheless pause impatiently to read an introduction such as this one, they are probably not aware of the change that has come over the writer in reading again the poems and the poet he is presenting. How often he has said to friends something like, "Oh, yes, Simon is so good, so very excellent. I call her the Queen of Metaphor. You should really read her." But having encountered the poems once again en masse, like hearing, say, Beethoven's quartets spaced out over a summer, he feels a wave of guilt wash over him because of his crude understatement, the laziness and superficiality of his easy praise. For he is stunned. Such brilliance, he thinks, such astounding music, such genius for the art and craft of metaphor. Such love for her people, and for the world despite its criminal inconsistencies and countless horrors. Why hasn't everyone read her? What can he say to convince them that they should? And so, this probably very inadequate but well-intentioned little essay. Please enjoy reading the remarkable poems of Maurya Simon.

—B. H. Fairchild (January 2016)

Questions My Daughters Asked Me,
Answers I Never Gave Them

1. What is love, how will we know it?

It's the thumbtack the bare foot martyrs itself to,
unleashing the blood-rich flames of autumn.
It is the cheek turned against the slap,
the executioner's gentle touch before the axe.
And you will know it by its circuitry of awe,
how it dazzles the mind, stunning the heart
into a fierce bleating.

2. Why is life so unfair?

Because the universe spins from chaos
in widening spirals, and people,
like electrons, are flung from the hand
of justice as freely as sparks
jettisoned from the sun.

3. How can we find our way in the wilderness?

Follow the little man with the foolish grin
who carries a lantern full of fireflies,
who becomes a dragon of purpose, a beacon
of laughter, who is your shadow's twin,
your angel of forgiveness, your desire.

4. Is there a God?

I don't know what the charts
and diagrams, the holy books,
the rapt prayers and curses,
the sudden miracles, can tell us.
I hear only the perfect silence
of a trillion stars . . .

5. What is the soul?

A thimbleful of light perhaps,
or the horizon's gold-singed spell;
maybe the dew-spangled jewels
shed by mourners; or perhaps
the shadow left shivering upon
water as a wild swan takes flight.

6. What lies beyond death?

A fever of unknowing, a match-head
struck in the darkness of the void.
A blue door without a handle
that suddenly swings open . . .

7. Who are you?

The voice of unreason and doubt,
the mother of exiles,
She-Who-Must-Not-Be-Obeyed,
the ravens' outcaste,
a painter of sighs,
your dream's amputation,
keeper of ancient longings,
the vessel of your first dawn,
a prophet without a tongue.

The Enchanted Room

"The evening sky to me is like
a window, and a lighted lamp,
and a waiting behind it."

—Rabindranath Tagore

The Sibyl

When I was a small girl of modest words, I thought
the fluted music rising up from under the hedgerows

to be no more than water traveling the roots, singing
over rocks as it moved silkily underground.

And those voices in the night, well, I believed
black swans had gathered in the garden font,

or thought perhaps the stars were chattering again
like a dawn procession of wives gone for the day's fish

to that market propped up at the horizon's gate.
Such sounds were the riddles of my youth, vague cures

for boredom while my brothers sailed their reed boats.
Now my days are littered with worries, despite the gold

light upon my arms, the masked adulation of priests.
For I know even Apollo's flattery couldn't save

Deiphobe from being strung up, finally, from a nail,
a captive in a bottle, condemned to wither into air.

Beloved of goats, what kind of lie is this I live?
Each prophecy I make is only a thimble of wisdom,

a sip of honey, one quick blink of clarity,
among a bewilderment of portents, omens, sighs.

Soon they will tire of me and cast me off like catgut
from a broken string. Nothing else sustains me now

but the rhythm of their prayers, the burning rain, darts
of their cold tongues upon my thighs, their fingertips

rousing my breasts, the forked melody of an aulos
splitting each night open, my body inflamed, my throat

thrown back as some god explodes from my lips, while
my own voice hides in the folds of my other mouth.

The Origin of Death

Once upon a time someone died. And because it was the first death, the universe was stunned; the trees in woods threw off their needle cloaks in dark despair, the many creatures, near and far, went into hiding behind clouds or under dry river-beds: the people, still a bit stiff in clay suits, remolded their faces to register fear. A woman had stretched herself out like a long canoe on the shore, had merely closed her eyes and closed her lungs to breath.

A child approached the cold body of the woman. "Mother," she said. "Wake up. It's time to bring in the flock." Someone in a bush nearby cleared his throat. Someone else felt, for the first time, the trickle of warm water leak from his eyes. An armadillo sniffed the woman, then laid down its head at her feet. "Mother," the child said again. And when for the third time the child addressed the woman and heard no answer, she walked away, down to the tide pools to gather shells.

This all happened so long ago that even fossils, with their hardy, imprinted stories, argue over the details. But it has been said things changed after that. Nervousness and impatience were soon born. Swallows migrated south in winter. Sharks grew sharp teeth. Bananas grew dark spots. And young armadillos thickened their hides. No one lived happily ever after, except the child, whose heart beats on, and who sees her mother in every stone.

The Soldier

They say my hands are machines,
oiled with blood.
They press me to guard the horizons,
to wash my hands with mud.
Taught not to question a cause,
just to die, my life becomes
a series of simple acts.

Keep your head empty, they say,
and your hair cut close to your scalp:
hide your birth marks so that the enemy
won't recognize you as himself.

I change the rules to fit my silence.
I carry the hope for a long life
at the bottom of my sagging heart.
My fingers aren't bullets, but vines;
and when I lean on my rifle at sunset
I feel like a farmer.

No one knows how I pay for doubt.
I try to measure everything I've done,
but in 18 years everything I've earned
is lint in my pockets.

Still, here I am, and how can I
confess my sins to come, knowing
that they will last forever?

What comes from my actions
is for the good of the world, they say.
And I try to love my destiny.

But I would rather be deceived, admit
I like my boots, and the rhythm of a march,
even the food, and the endless jokes
about the colonel's tiny prick.

They tell me, oil your machines,
keep them clean.

But the truth of the matter is:
their eyes don't cry,
their hearts have dried up
like severed figs,
and to ask them for reasons
would be like asking a dying man
what time it is.

Tooth Fairy

On her wedding night, my mother
flattened herself into a needle
which my father then threaded
by drawing himself through its eye,
disappearing into the darkness of her body.
Then my mother hurled herself up
into the sky and hooked her hair
on the moon's nail.

Thus I was born both
out of that tranquility to which she
marooned herself, and out of an essence
of loss, that one-armed bandit.

I'm a beautiful sight:
a diadem of stars nests in my hair,
and my breasts are immaculate.
My eyes search the world's windows
for tiny boxes, handkerchiefs,
or bottles stashed under countless pillows.

A certain tautness around the lips,
a tension in the fist,
tell me which children wait
on the edge of sleep for my visit.
I burrow my hand under their heads
and deftly extract what I need.
Grateful, I bend and kiss their pursed lips.
After tossing the teeth in my sack,
I flex my wings and rise

through the curtains, like a moth
chased by the flame of greed.

It's no secret what I do with the teeth:
I implant them in the mouths
of prophets, so their words forever
remain small, pure, unfinished.

Snails

We've broken out the eggshells again,
and leave a trail of them, jagged triangles,
whitening the garden's border.
Now, at night, from the kitchen window,
we see the moon, narrowed to a Cheshire grin,
conspiring with the snails, scything
out a path between radishes and marigolds.

If only we had McQueen's valor
in the face of the faceless Blob,
or the Frenchman's aptitude and appetite
for garlic and butter; if only we weren't so proud
and could congratulate such fierce hunger.
But we have had them dead-drunk from beer,
or puckered into tiny fists, cruelly salted.

Eggshells are a fragile last resort
against these night riders who wear
the spirals of the ocean on their backs,
who peer from twin periscopes as they hunt
for the first green lights. Quiet as moss, calm,
devoted: they travel the ground open-mouthed,
dragging shoelaces of light behind them.

Tat Tvam Asi

Above us the awakening sky grows warm,
the moon's crescent horn blows itself dim:

a Tamil fisherman poles his *kaṭṭumarām*
across a flight of clouds.

With its slim neck and face open as a child's,
the Bay of Bengal lays its head down in Adyar

in this lagoon with its teak pavilions
and dwarfed Casuarina pines flush on the banks.

Two egrets, their legs dangling like sticks of incense,
trail smoky lines in the clear black water.

Perhaps Yeats in a cream-colored shirt
would have paused here once with Annie Besant

to marvel at the flocks of birds spangling
the horizon with mango-red wings,

or she, gripping the balsa rail, seeing the clouds'
turbans unravel in spools of silk, would have smiled.

There in the water's pasture our images
shift from foot to foot and fracture

while we hang motionless above the water's eye,
our bodies two shadows on a bridge.

This is the year I'd step out of myself
if I could, barefoot and without a passport,

arriving at this place, an infinitesimal ache
pressing its lips to my throat,

the sky's bowl of alms emptying itself into water,
the water's opus of light opening like a lotus.

The Bearer's Son

Sundaram has stopped telling us
about the "coconut lid" on his hut,
how the rain rushes down
through palm fronds
in dirty waterfalls of light.

On a mat in the Harijan *cērri*
his son burned himself up with fever,
crying Ammā! and Rām!

Now, twelve hours later,
the funeral pyre pours its smoke
and sparks of bone
into the rose-watered air.
Bearing a gash of vermillion
and a blade of ash on his brow,
Sundaram weeps as he walks
along the rising river.

In Madras, monsoons repeat
themselves when no one is listening.
Droughts come and go
like missionaries bent
on conversion of the soil.
Children, named and loved,
their pockets empty, die of fever.

Eyes compressed, Sundaram returns:
his son's voice clenched in his teeth.

Next winter he will firewalk
across a road tiled with red coals
as a penance to God.
And in his blood, year
after year, Sundaram
rehearses the dissolution
of the world.

Harijan cērri: *Dalit village*
Ammā, Rām: *Mother, God*
Madras: *Chennai*

Firewalking

A long strand of stars appears tonight
in the branches of the flame tree.

The moon, waking now from its eastern bed,
glides over the coals in a silver cloud of smoke.

The women go first with their palms raised
and their eyes glazed with love and their mouths

open slightly as if parted for a kiss. Then,
a flurry of adolescent girls, their saris

lifted above the knee, tucked into waistbands.
Some hold babies above their heads, and strangely,

the babies are quiet, even solemn, as they lift
their chins away from the incomprehensible heat.

Many are weeping now, weeping in joy,
in grief: old men who remember dancing above

the white ashes and who saw the goddess appear
with her necklace of skulls, with her six arms

beckoning them onward across past lives—and now
children whose tears trail amber lines on their skin.

Now a hush as the men tighten their dhotis
over their narrow hips and two from the temple

drag the goat squealing and baaing to the end
of the red glowing pit, and one throws up his arm

and the long blade falls swiftly through the neck
of the animal, and the goat's head rolls.

The old women take the head, take the body away.
And the sound begins to grow again, a chanting,

a frenzy of devotion, a swelling of joy; sweat
covers their bodies in jeweled nets and their flesh

is so red, their blood so red, their voices rising
with the smoke, and their bodies, rapt with love,

form a string of dark pearls over the fiery coals,
and nothing pains them, nothing, nothing at all.

Madras Insomnia

Struck head-on by the wind's blow,
two trees hum like tuning forks.
The sky's colander drains off
water from the stars while a parrot
sharpens its voice. A lone peacock
sputters in the dark.

I can't sleep under the fan's blades.
Saffron geckos cling upside-down,
chirping and chirping for gnats.
Mosquitoes unzip themselves from the wall.
Even the bee-eaters' slender tongues
untie their knots.

Outside, a banyan tree sinks its hooks
into an acre of dust. In the blue hills
langurs leaf through green crops,
and water buffalo sink into mud.
Spirals of light cling to night's ribs.
White ants spill out of bark.

I wish for the sleep of clear rivers,
for the midnight dreams of saints.
I wait to enter another realm where
one flame dances eternally on one toe:
where the bride of heaven sings a single note,
and the king cobra's hood cups the world.

Epitaph

Remember the black confetti
of sparrows released into clouds,

and the swivel-headed mantis
rotating its eyes like a madman;

remember the uprooted sapling
leaving its invisible claw in earth,

the double helix of lives
that vanishes with the scythe;

remember a thousand little bells
singing like river angels,

the heaving galaxies lifting
sequins of water from girls' eyes,

and the pollen of plundered bone
shifting its footprints underground.

Days of Awe

"I am filled with love,
as a great tree with wind,
as a sponge with the ocean,
as a great life with suffering,
as time with death."

—Anna Swir

Clothes That Wear Me

1. Dress

One day the voices of twenty women
singing a Gregorian chant caused a dress
to materialize out of thin air.
It fit me perfectly, and even buttoned itself
in front, without my having to lift a finger.
When I went down the street in this dress
men fell to their knees, sparrows stopped
their small talk to follow me.
The zipper in the back sang "Ave Maria,"
and the pockets were lined with lilies.
Oh my dress full of ballads,
my dress that accepted me like a flask—
how could I lose you that night
I gambled with those young men
and their loaded dice?

2. Winter Cloak

I've taken the selfishness of men
and sewn a winter cloak out of it.
Its holes are the size of small towns
with storms hovering over them.
I can never iron out its wrinkles,
so I toss it into the furnace where,
naturally, it refuses to burn.
I'm stuck with wringing out its tears.

It's true, from chin to ankle I'm weak.
I can only say "no" on odd days;
I weep over the deaths of spiders,
those asterisks on the staircase.
But my mind, my sanitarium of a mind,

has the strength of three thousand
infantrymen planting geraniums
in the desert. Such strength
recedes when I wear my angry coat,
my barren coat, my coat that
absorbs my life like a sponge.

3. *Favorite Things*

My favorite bra is bright blue.
One cup is larger than the other
so that my heart has room to expand.
This bra speaks now and then.
It abhors Neo-Expressionism,
black underwear, florescent lights.
Lately it's been encouraging me
to become a wet nurse to mankind.
My bra argues for divine love,
the milk of human kindness.
It's quickly falling out
of my favor.

My favorite shoe is shaped like a book.
When I put my right foot into it

I become a great, golden Buddha
pulling gently on my earlobes—
suddenly I can read the whole,
miraculous world in a glance.
When I put my left foot into it
I shrink down to a water beetle.

Then I scurry in between the litter
of words, circumventing commas
and periods, and rowing through
the silences on each page.

4. Veils

Far away my dead children
are putting on their veils.

First they press them with tiny irons,
then they hold them up to the light.

Taking turns, the three infants tie
diaphanous veils around each other's heads.

When they wear their veils they see
everything that ever was or will be.

When they lift off their veils they cry.
For them, eternity is inexplicably sad.

As a mother of exiles, I never loved these children,
though I cried when my body turned them out.

Now they gather their flocks of stones,
as a chandelier of rain hangs over them.

Their veils are clouded with longing;
their faces were made to shine.

Breakwater

Under the huge, oily, half-barnacled rocks,
my sister and I fished every Saturday for crabs.
We lived to see them foam wildly at the mouth,
their curved claws clacking like pinking shears
against the fabric of their fear, their nubby eyes
black-stemmed and blind, searching for ours.
We hated and loved them zealously, as we did
the sand sharks who wore grim faces on their backs;
the jellyfish, with their colonies of purple barbs;
the helpless grunion dying in phosphorescent glory;
the riptides that, over the years, carried us
miles from shore. All the dangers of the ocean
beckoned to us back then, just as our mother called
out our sweet names, so as to spell us into being.
It was danger we thought we longed for,
more than love; for love seemed always dry-
docked, a dead end, whereas the sea-slung wind
was heavy with mystery as it swept in whiffs
of pirate ships, bloodied rags, sirens, and tar.
Those nights we slipped out my sister's window,
climbed down the wooden siding of the second floor,
alighted on bicycles, flew off in our nightgowns
down the empty esplanade to King Harbor;
those nights we climbed the breakwater, leaping
like ghosts in darkness from rock to rock,
as waves boiled over our toes: we had to hold on
to each other's waist to keep from diving in.
Leap, leap the spindrift spat out at us,
the thrumming swells undulating their bellies
over the closed womb of the blackened water.

Something in the fast-moving clouds overhead
made us listen to our own breathing; something
vast and ageless, like an old grief ever singing
its salt in our veins: the ocean calling us home.

Boy Crazy

I used to watch the roses loosen
their pink wigs as I clocked the rain.
One-two, one-two, the drops plunked
the petals down into the gutter.
Drenched, I strolled my way into town
hoping to meet the boy I shuddered
to think of, the boy with hair black
as patent leather, the boy with a sneer
and cigarette clamped between his lips.
I was feverish with innocence, my skin
aglow, my shadow almost voluptuous.
Past the blue houses and an old Volvo
backfiring from an alley, past
The Lighthouse where once Dizzy Gillespie
had blown me a kiss when I was twelve,
past the Mermaid Restaurant where I first
saw my father flirt with a fierce waitress,
I finally made my way to the pier.
Only one fisherman crouched near a pail
of squid, and his hair was yellow.
The sound of rain was swallowed by waves
pounding the shore with white fists.
Over Catalina Island a rainbow perched
like a tweezed eyebrow raised in surprise.
I kept track of how late he was,
while clouds paired up on the horizon,
and the minutes drifted into the surf
like bits of torn paper.
But, he came, after all. Dizzy, elated,
faint with restraint, I played it cool.

Kiss me, kiss me, he whispered, sneering
his powerful sneer as he bent over me,
his thin hands cupping the two blades
of my shoulders. Hot ice was what I felt—
a melting and stiffening, a strange tug
in my thighs, blood rushing everywhere.
He had to go home at last, and so did I.
But I stayed and swayed on the pier,
to watch the wing-rowing pelicans pause
in mid-air before they released themselves
from their bodies' bows, and dove
into the amethyst waters below.

Dream Babies

Double-chinned or fine-fingered,
web-toed, chagrined malingerers,
despoilers of diapers, night
balkers, day squawkers:
a bounty of babies visits me.
They coo like miniature muses,
their tongues wet, petulant fuses;
they snap at my dry nipples,
those poor doorbells, my dead eyes
rising to their open mouths
like anxious buttons.
How my uterus tightens now,
shrinks to a triangular diamond,
how my cervix snickers.
Why do they come nightly,
this army of whimperers,
this hungry parade, beating
their rattles against my ribcage,
tearing off their bibs?
Take us, take us, they beg,
butter our chins with love,
this-little-piggy our fingers.
This can't go on much longer.
The honeycombs are overfilled
with larvae, the bees drag
their pollen-powdered legs
over the garden, the anthills
swarm with soldiers, the dead
gather in the darkroom.

For Naomi

Last night you sleepwalked down the stairs,
dressed in your nakedness as a candle is
in its own glow. Perhaps you answered the sound
of wind dragging its chains through the trees,
or merely were caught by the moon's pull.
Whatever it was, you surprised me awake:
for your body, that early lily, lit up the stairwell.
I thought, where did my child go?

I thought of the rings of Jupiter, confusion
of lights, all the bands of love around your life.
I thought of Grandma Rose, whose nakedness
once startled me as a child into terror,
to think one so brittle might still allure.

And I wanted to cover your small shoulders
with the armor of my body, or with
an awkwardness people turn away from
calmly, as from the ordinary.
I wanted to dream you into a sanctuary
where no one could stray but the pure of heart.
I took your hand and led you up the stairs,
though even in that double darkness,
your body was already divining its way.

Contusion

The fraction of a second it took
to sever the thin white cord, that
vessel that carries off your seed,
I saw the doctor's hands perform
their legerdemain under the spot-
light, and you groggy as a sailor,
shipwrecked, cast ashore, sat up
to see the blue testis exposed,
your thighs trembling so wildly:
the body's spasm of despair.

He was too nervous for comfort,
the doctor whose son committed
suicide by laying himself down
on steel ties, a sacrifice to
the gods of locomotion, though
why he sweated while you poked
through your shroud of Seconal
has always made me doubt him,
as if to legitimize my brusque calm
he needed to be perfect.

Though eight years have passed,
and our daughters have doubled
themselves in our delight,
that scene reappears so solidly
it seems an intaglio of memory;
and I see again and again your
inconsolable loss, so subtly

hidden by your pride, how your
jaw grew tight as a current
of light in you switched off.

Theme and Variations

What is dark and oblique in a face—
eclipses under the eyes, the throat's blackness
pushing against the teeth, pupils welling up
with midnight, cobwebs and crow's feet
penned deftly with thin ink, a sunken sadness
in the cheeks or brow—such things teach us
how, millimeter-by-millimeter, pain seeps
into our tenderest disquietude. And just as
our breath heaves us in and out of ourselves,
just as the good muscles stretch and contract,
as the heart storms and calms itself perpetually,
so the face wears both sides, day and night,
on its skin, becomes both prison and garden.

My face nears forty now
and begins to play with new shadows.
They must crop up from beneath the light,
strange blooms that thrive blindly.
Now I approach the mirror as a confidante,
with the deliberation of a Solomon gone dim,
with the fecund look of a stagnant pond,
with an air that hangs with the weight of loss,
lifeless as a smudge of oil on parchment.
And when I question it, my mirror answers me:
Yes, childhood is just a dream your body devised.
Or, *You are a stone, a canvas, a wild*
and abandoned place without walls.

Survival

I keep the scorpion, *Vaejovis spinigerus*,
in a Mason jar filled with delicate corpses.
The carpenter ant has curled dryly into itself;
the white fairy moth is poised in death—
a tiny airplane that nose-dived, collapsed;
even the long-necked Raphidia lapsed
into motionlessness, stung to the quick.
This scorpion earns respect for keeping a wick
of breath lit, despite my cold, antagonistic eye.
But what of all these other creatures high
and low in jars, boxes, aquariums, and cages?
Two frogs, in two months, have, in stages,
grown depressed and starved themselves to death.
And two infant deer mice with huge heads
refuse to suckle on the milk-doused Q-tip
I offer them; they, too, have begun to slip.
In every cranny and nook hosts of dying wings,
while the scorpion crooks his ready sting.
Only he and the hot-blooded hamster thrive:
the one feasting like a saint on sacrifice,
the other frantically spinning out the nights,
something electric keeping her alive.

King Midas's Daughter

She retires to the tower, her only haven
away from the artless glare of gold.
Weighted down with plums and a melon
not yet hardened by her father's hold,
she mounts the stone stairs, her steps fierce,
her long red hair uncoiling from its spiral.
From the window the far waves break in tiers;
he will not touch them, he is too fearful
to leave his glowing world, his golden throne.
Against the curved blade of the horizon,
she sees a ship with fluttering sails blown
dangerously close to the harbor: *Don't come*,
she silently commands it, and it goes.

She is like a plant calling for water.
She is like a fist pounding a pillow.
She's forgotten the taste of her own laughter,
and the sound of a mockingbird in the willow.
She sees him below in a garden among statues
which are grotesque, familiar, golden.
And he's calling up to her now: *Come choose
a flower, any flower!* And his foolish exuberance
makes her jump from her chair and rush to him,
wanting to shake this curse from his shoulders,
wanting to hug his thinning body, unloosen
its cold grief, its sorrow of greed, however
he scolds her, or dazzles her into silence.

Madras Lament

All night the night watchman pounds his stick
against the rust-red dirt of our road.
And curled against the papaya's display,
a pi-dog snores, half her golden fur gone
from asafoetida or mange. Off in the distance
peacocks wail, clouds rearrange themselves
in a flotilla of sails whitening the horizon.

I am up, as usual, at this hour, filling
my mind with the fan's arithmetic, the sighs
issuing from other rooms, the busy quiet.
Somewhere, beyond Egmore District, the sound
of a night train travels the darkness;
and from the direction of Mount Road, I hear
a monkey's chatter, the angry retort of a crow.

I've spent a year of wakefulness in this bed,
awaiting some midnight revelation.
June's monsoon has come and gone, leaving
behind a million silver holes in the road.
Life's balanced between known and unknown,
between the thwacks of a watchman's stick
and the dusty clatter of far-off hooves.

I slip out of the mosquito netting again
to pad across the cool marble to the balcony.
A terrible beauty shines from the stars,
as if the lies of time re-gild their petals.
I think it's loss that's wrung me out:
my lover an ocean beyond bullock carts,
night-blooming jasmine, and the starving

asleep in their rags, their palms frozen
open like cups, their closed faces aglow,
their shadows pooled into ochre stains.
But I'm wrong: it's the approaching light,
hastening like another storm toward the city,
that pierces me to this surrender,
that makes me cry out for such splendor.

Speaking in Tongues

"The poet is the priest of the invisible."

—Wallace Stevens

Origins

I.

It has ended as it had begun,
in the twilight of each earmarked page,

where the reader eavesdrops on himself,
the deep hunger of his life laid mercilessly bare,

and all the metaphors for desire nothing
but platitudes and fingerprints, a harvest of sighs.

But it wasn't always so: once, long before
the page peeled itself, keening, from the tree,

there was stone, gray as a brain cell, smooth
as the palm of a hand, and there was an awl

bent and straightened and fired to a point,
palpable and heavy with intention, with portent.

Let us imagine ourselves there, on the periphery
of dawn, a flock of wild ducks rising quietly

in a chevron overhead, the cleared marsh
cobbled with shadows, the sincere lizards poised

for defeat, the pit smoke navigating its flags:
all of nature's operators attentive to the hour.

A pile of gnawed bones, a stern architecture,
the first and last tenement of worms,

occupies a pocket of the imagination, as does
the distant song of the hunters who are calling

for forgiveness from the spirit of the bear.
Tadpoles glisten like obsidian in the shadows,

a ganglion of roots edges out of the water's lips,
a glimpse of catfish whiskers beckons,

but the scribe sits motionless on her rock,
another rock aproned to her lap, an infant

with twitching mouth, sated and sleep-weary,
lies cradled in his hollowed stump.

Like her, we are mute, invisible scribes
to history, invisible to each other and ourselves.

II.

We would want her to tell us everything
about her gods, those dead and living,

those to whom she will offer her child
in the mayhem of the full moon, after

the rains have betrayed them once again,
flooding their stockpile of gooseberries, nuts.

We would want her to write with menstrual blood
the tale of the roasted man, the tale

of lightning, the story of subterranean stars
planted with lice in the burial grounds,

the long epic of the three-eyed cousin,
that traveler with his treasure of cures and curses,

who danced with buckthorns strapped to his soles,
who turned himself into an eagle, who,

with ginger clamped between his black teeth,
foresaw a future of armies, a future beyond

imagination, when the cold descended forever
and their voices became mere scratchings in ice.

But the sprawl of spring is upon the fields.
Deer mice plough through parsnip and eelgrass,

a decomposing weasel stares up fixedly
into the burls of besotted clouds as the sun

drags its drizzling gold above the jagged crowns.
She lives only in this moment, while we,

in our armchairs and Saturday shoes,
inhabit present and past, the dialectic

of the dial, the pull of gravity's wheel
turning us this way and that, like dashes

between clauses, like a meniscus upon the horizon.
We are a frontier beyond her memory. So,

she picks up a stone and hits it obliquely
against the awl and bites the first notch

into the smooth, sullen slate of granite.
She knocks and bangs out the first word:

a stick-figure man, his penis shafted downward,
a thick finger pointing to earth.

III.

Where does such musing lead the muser?
Pen and paper, purpose and failure,

the dithyrambic songs of an errant dreamer:
all is illusion, all is yearning.

Each moment musters eternity, as if all voices—
here in the telepathy of the lover's grief,

in the unspooled cry of the lying sycophant,
in the polysyllabic oratory of the fool—

are ramblings that culminate in silence.
Must we memorize only songs without lyrics?

Should we grasp only the straws of unknowing?
The world exclaims itself in the sprung rhythms

of the stream, in the brief, aortal currents
of a million pantomimes, in the din of decay;

we are, each of us, one notch carved deeply,
effortlessly into the continuum of time.

Later scribes will say they knew something of us,
of our minuets and misfortunes, our fear.

For some truth always lyres the lips,
some urge to perpetuate even the starkest,

the oldest, most misspent outpouring arises:
being, itself, pools like dew upon the tongue.

And the woman, with her encouraged hand,
calloused and blunt-fingered, graceless,

feels what, in lonely times, we call
the Muse, spiraling out from groin, from heart,

quickening in her veins, unfurling in the lines
of her awkward palm, pulsing, pulsing like fire.

She cocks her head, listening to the rich buzz
of blood in her eardrums, and she laughs.

IV.

When they return from the far forests,
their spidery beards are long, and their hard feet,

scrupulously clean, bear the ocher circles-
within-circles of success; the charcoal petals,

like paw prints, climb the trellis of their legs.
The bear's eyeless head is massive and fierce,

its odor thick upon the air, its mauve tongue
split by a spearhead, its penis and testicles

garlanded, strung by sinews, around the neck.
They make an altar and they build a bonfire

that reaches skyward, trailing a fountain of stars,
as the sun ossifies the sunken shadows into dust.

Days ago the men ate the heart, lungs, spleen,
the powerful liver, the knowing eyes, the stomach.

Now they all feast on the good flesh,
the grease slicking their forearms white.

She wants to show them her word, the one
she labored over while the infant slept

and the others braided rushes into baskets,
while the half-grown children chanted carefully

to the fireflies to come out of hiding,
or rehearsed the solstice in their fathers' furs.

But she hesitates. History dotes on such
hesitations; it feeds off such hesitations.

Perhaps it was enough merely to commit
herself to that one utterance, just as

we impose ourselves upon the earth, commit
ourselves earnestly, steadfastly, without

obeisance to cause and effect, without dispute
from gods, and with a graceful, numb certainty.

The smoke rises above the skewered limbs,
the carbon arch above them dotted with pinpricks

of light, and the wind slings a cloak of moisture
over their radiant circle, haloing each of them.

The woman slips her hand under her belly-cloth,
where she has worn the heavy slab against her skin

until the heaviness of the word entered her womb,
until that heaviness came to weigh upon her

like a man lying upon her belly, like the world,
itself, entering her, making her solid as stone.

Here, she says at last. *Here is a picture,*
a word for us. Here is the spirit-of-man.

V.

Do we write ourselves into the world
merely to defy our own mortality, or is there

some equation of anguish, an integer of joy,
that charges us to frame ourselves in language

that we might merge ourselves with that simple-
minded psyche some call God?

Impossible, lofty, foolhardy ambitions.
How small each voice's tenor; yet each is greater

than the zero whining at the base of the skull,
greater than the silence of the dead, who,

with their pinched lips and fallen faces,
fume in their prisons, awaiting the Word.

Touch us, we want to say, *touch us into meaning*.
If only we could leap from our genes, repudiate

each cruel inheritance that leads us astray, that
leads us to collective lessons that only confound.

Let us be Eve, Adam again, or Gilgamesh,
that we might begin anew, rewrite the garden's

perimeters, reclaim our favorite dark.
Though all the old myths entertain us with defeat

or triumph—Moses with his sacred ark of laws;
Hercules hewing out a claim for superhuman will;

Pandora with her paltry greed, her errors;
Cronos, sad cannibal of his own domestic galaxy;

Kali dancing on demons while she juggles
with death, her fangs glistening their seductions;

even Paul Bunyan, Johnny Appleseed, Batman,
and all the rest with their skullduggery or magic—

what do the old myths mean now? What?
The post-literate, twentieth-century mind knows

too well how to refine chaos, how to define
loss in terms of decimals, gain in terms of pleasure.

The question of meaning answers itself
with a split tongue, paradoxically:

all is meaningless; all is fraught with meaning.
Like stars we write ourselves into the black pages.

VI.

She has awakened abruptly from a dream.
Maybe because it is bright under the scalloped moon,

and the ripples off the lake reflect a parade of stars,
or perhaps because the child has begun to suck

again, and floods his mother's body with sudden
wetness, the warm, sharp urine soaking her hair;

whatever the cause, she pries the pursed lips off
her nipple and lays the child in another's arms.

An owl lifts itself out of the night-gathering marsh,
its wings beating only inches above her head.

She studies a pile of broken femurs, thonged sticks,
debris strewn about the clearing like a healer's cache.

The dream rears up before her in a piercing light
and with a chemical clarity: she is alone, walking

up a mountain that is violently steep, deeply barren.
When she reaches the summit she sees a dwelling

shaped like the termites' conical tower, only huge,
decorated with cowrie shells, blue jay feathers, bits

of broken bark, swatches of snakeskin, porcupine quills,
burrs, thistles, strings of red berries, and flints.

She wonders why she hasn't a name, something
to hold between her teeth like a seed, a charm.

And where are the others? Where the drum
of the moon with its hollow chord, where

the legions of stirrings under pebbles, or above them
in this strange paralysis of night? Where are the gods?

Trembling, she sings out to the unnatural darkness
as she enters the cleft in the mud tower,

as she passes through the door of one world
into the mysterious shadow of another.

Together we enter with her: it is easy for us
to extinguish our fear, to disallow the dead

within us who spur us toward danger;
for we obey oblivion's drowsy enticements

because we may so effortlessly close the pages
of the past, so nimbly turn to the pinwheels of light

that call us forth, like starving fish,
to the bait of the present tense.

She enters, we enter. Whirlpooling embers burn
before her, red pupils dilating into wounds:

an eagle-headed thing! Four fur-matted breasts
dangle huge snakes clamped to each nipple,

then a furious beating of wings, the beast's talons
brandishing bundles of spirit blades, its beak

screaming out flames, enormous bull thighs pumping
the swollen ground, the genitals male, female,

frothing, dripping, spawning an uproar of voices,
the monster lowering its head toward her, its mouth

a firestorm, its nostrils volcanoes, its eyes—
but they are her own eyes, her eyes!

VII.

She has been squeezing the gourd so tightly
that it breaks open, spilling lake water over her.

The dream vanishes into a coyote's cry, evaporates
like a spore of spring snow on her thumb.

Now the moon is achingly near, taut and burnished,
as it grazes the cattails, the calla lilies.

It is her fault, she knows, her failure.
For she has forgotten to place herself, her body,

in her own universe, forgotten to articulate
her breath into the contours of stone, of memory.

Now she attires herself in bracken, picks up the awl,
the belly-board of stone; she will begin again.

She bangs a convenient stone against the rock-page,
nicking out minute chunks of grain: first the long,

vertical line of torso, then the horizontal arms;
the spread legs follow, and between them, the vulva,

her second mouth that calls to the earth like a lover.
She makes the breasts vast, pendulous, great teardrops

balanced over the rim of the world, over the belly-mound.
And it is finished. She moves her tongue's tip

into the cool grooves and gulleys, tasting an eloquence
there, a sweetness as powerful as a god's name.

And when she returns to the hypnosis of sleep,
to the unfinished dream with its unfinished voices,

she will feel her bones compose themselves again,
feel her baby's beetle-small breath tattoo her skin;

and never will she imagine that eighty thousand moons
will rise and set before the same images of man and woman

are inscribed upon a slate with such delicacy and hope,
with such mournful love, such urgency and fear.

She will not imagine the bubble-shaped, metal bird
hurtling past the Milky Way with its encapsulated couple,

rocketing into orbit like a holy relic, like a prayer,
plunging into the bottomless dark with its gift.

VIII.

Things end as they begin, in the brief pauses
between beats, in the breath that fuels

all incantations—the flutter-tonguings
we hear now only in the bloom of our deaths,

or in the glossary of our births, and in the still,
blank places in the mind, between rooms, stanzas,

where time gnaws on its bones and all is pure energy—
things begin as they end: in a freewheeling spiral.

How then to pull free and yet stay harnessed?
We must keep to the page, with its magnetic forces:

it's the deep bed we lay down in to dream
beyond ourselves; it is yet another ocean

out of which we crawl with our knotted tails,
with our slim gills, our flimsy fins.

We must carry our words within the pouch
of each heartbeat, not as loose change but

as diamonds, fiery-faceted, hardened by terror,
dangerous with power, radioactive with magic.

Like the scribe exposing her words to her world,
fearful of every cut in the flesh, every scar,

fearful that the ancient affections of the gods
will be withdrawn, like her we must gather our senses.

We must wear the world like a necklace, a noose,
around our throats, our bent ribcages expanding

with the emptiness of uninhabited hours;
we must fill with insurgency, swell with riddles,

be heroes without legends, ones equipped with spears
etched by tooth marks, ones whose burdens of stone

lie like pillows under our heads, whose low croons
echo in the eddies of time, in the whorls of air.

Here, in the unanswered clutch of longings that
darken in us even as they illumine our lives,

lie the letters of all our bewildered alphabets.
Evening fades into morning, morning into noon;

a hundred carpenters on the horizon rebuild midnight.
All the lines on the palm of the page converge

to form the one word respoken from mouth to mouth
like a blessing, like a kiss, so deftly it's inscribed

in common flesh—that word issued by God or god, that
breath that speaks us, that we speak: *Oh, animus.*

The Golden Labyrinth

I think of Rousseau's jungle odalisque—
the black-haired woman's skin so white
it stops the heart—and somewhere, near
the edge of consciousness, a crouching tiger
waits almost as languidly as she, waits for
that urgent darkness deeper than any art.

—from "Nagarahole"

Want

There are too many names here for suffering,
too many faces of want, be they human or not.

A bullock, frothing at the mouth, gets whipped
again by his driver; an armless child begs

with his feet; a battered wife picks up a knife.
Where can this pain flow, but into the heart

and back out, grimy, twisted into black knots?
I understand Buddha's dharma now, his silent

disavowal of a world so laden with our tears
it overflows like sludge from a polluted tap.

He joined the forests' maze to meditate for years
upon a seamless, carbon void of namelessness,

to lose his identity there. For him, despair first
engendered loss, then gain of selflessness,

and then, at last, an uplifting into sparks—
I see him on every road, completely naked

but for his decaying loincloth and wormy bowl;
I see his matted hair, his lice-infested beard.

He is whole now, holy, yet empty of what
drives my hand to write—utterly empty of want.

Dharma

Shortly after dawn they arrive: first, sullen Ramiza,
who tilts to the weight of her plastic satchel,

her gap-toothed mouth a frowning scythe,
an unnamed grief tarnishing her gaze.

Daily, Sahib's marble kitchen awaits her,
its pots primly lined up like docile convent girls,

its rainbowed spices richly smoldering in jars: stars
of anise, turmeric, cayenne, fenugreek, and cardamom.

Now Ibrahim legs stiffly down Aliasker Road Cross.
Thin as a muezzin's predawn cry, gaunt-cheeked,

he plods to the gate in his pinched, black shoes:
an agéd man, draft-wary, his right eye gone out.

Yawning, Abdul Gaffar salutes the day watchman—
"Salaam alekum," and "Alekum salaam," Ibrahim replies,

as he doffs his Musselman cap, then settles down
to another day of fitful dozing beneath the tamarind.

And how soon the shrunken "Ayah" bends to her tasks.
Her face is a precinct of wrinkles, her tattooed arms

so brittle one would think they'd collapse under
the weight of her sodden bundles, trays of brass.

As sweeper, she briskly chases off the lint and dust,
squinting, coughing, her small feet splayed out.

She nods to Zuleka, "the stout one," arriving now
an hour late, her bun already slightly unstrung,

her flimsy sari unkempt, her choli riding too high
upon her breasts, her voice charged by reprimands.

She stations herself over our granite washing slab, then
flails each garment high above her head, slapping it down

hard upon the sudsy rock, over and over again.
An eon of days stream past as the servants labor,

their every act tediously polished, then repeated, then
rephrased by season after season—as the tamarind's pods

twirl and drop, as mynahs scream insults at a cat,
as the earth spins in circles on its tilted axis.

I watch them from another world, privileged and
unspent here by the rigors of doing others' chores,

and I see how every ordered gesture of their lives,
how their eagerness to serve their wealthy Sahib

(whose life shines amid theirs like a distant star),
how every step they take, every pot that's stirred and

washed and stored, every bow they make becomes
a measure of devotion to Allah's invisible rewards.

Karma

Whomever you want to be, you can be,
my mother said, year in and out, her vow
a litany of doctor-lawyer-Indian chief.
She was wrong to think only of bright deeds
and lives, of limelight, accolades, fattened days.
For when I see the leper on the road, misshapen,
scabrous, wheeling his gnarled body dark with pain,
I know my own easy health, my unclever luck
for gain are even more ephemeral than Self.
Reincarnate, I become what's most loath to me:
palsied whore, brutish pimp, murderer, pariah.
Limitless the roles I could assume, Mother,
when my back is spun like a turnstile of fate,
when the appalling strangers I meet are myself.

Leah in the Vale of Tears

She hates the way men stare at her,
their eyes narrowed by desire,
and then the obscene jokes directed
toward her breasts, her golden hair.
She abhors seeing foot-long rats
stretched out sleekly by death, and
the steaming piles of human shit
we sidestep, and the toothless beggars
who smile as they clutch her shirt.
Day after day, I see a new horror
registered upon her lovely face;
a new despair blossoms on her skin.
And she has learned an inwardness
of pain that bends her tender body
like a cupped palm around a flame.
And now her seldom-heard laughter
sounds bereft of innocence, mirth.
At thirteen, she understands so much—
hunger, desperation, being voiceless,
the burdens each of us must bear.

The Ugly Dog

Because it was sweltering and I was rushing
from market to stationer's to bookstore to bank,

because I was tired of noise and my foreign face,
because the diesel-choked streets made me faint

and hungry for my distant mountains, my family,
because I was sick of the world, sick of my spirit

flagging like a flea-bitten sheet behind me—
I was slow to notice your hideous shadow

trailing my heels—what I took at first sight
to be a fallen gargoyle, so unearthly you looked,

so terribly misshapen, your tongue drooling blood,
your pink body covered in blistering sores.

"Shoo!" I said in my sternest, raspiest voice,
"get lost, scram, get out of here, go home!"

But you tipped back your battle-scarred ears,
wouldn't budge an inch—I think you sneered—

cast down your one good eye instead,
and stood stock-still by my side.

For hours you haunted my steps like Anubis,
guard dog from Egypt's Otherside, a frescoed-

over plaster face, moldy and crumbling, staring
past the black grief of kings and queens without

as much as a whine: you wouldn't be turned aside.
You followed me like some perfectly trained stud,

a pedigree who loves his mistress with an iron will—
for hours you escorted me, heeling like a champion,

from Queen's Market to the Bengali Sweet Shop,
from bus stop to the tailor's, and all the while

I hissed "Out!" at you and "Po!" in a hoarse voice,
in my most righteous Anglo-Tamil, to no avail.

I hid for an hour in an ice cream parlor, but you again
triumphed, wagging your bald tail once as I emerged.

I gave up at last. You'd won. You knew something
I could only surmise: perhaps we'd been conspirators

in our past lives? My smell (your smell) provocative
perhaps, or repellent, addictive? Maybe, I thought,

you aren't even real: nothing so ugly survives.
I know now how most you shamed and exposed me,

how you made of my biased humanity a paltry thing:
I feared you in your grotesque form for your love

of me, brief as it was, for your seeing in my face
a counterpart to your loneliness, a companion

stranger, another outcast—a creature who needed
your guidance to return from her deadened life.

Alex in Hindustan

Talmudic men, you'd call them—
those ancient sadhus in peach
who daven to the tame wind.

Submit, you'd tell me, to all
that bewilders you, or be
revamped as the Jagannātha,

juggernaut, lord of the world,
master of the word, and bow
to no one, with a smileless smile.

Be extreme as that poor man
whose sustenance is a hope
suspended upon nothing.

Your face is your bowl:
go begging with it full
of the soft grains of love.

And you dance before me
as you talk, a ghostly man
laughing with white teeth.

But there is no one here,
Alex, and the Indian sun
raises a cruel blister

on my heart, and when
the dumb night descends,
and the moon like a sponge

dampens my forehead,
I must ask you again—
return, return from the dead.

Banded Krait

Thin as a licorice whip
looped with tiny wedding bands,
she slides across our path,
inviting a betrothal with chance.
"Seven-step snake,"
the Tamils call her reverently.
For after she strikes,
it's a short walk to death.

Why the slender fangs curving
into slivers of ice?
Why such numbing venom pouched
in that slight, lovely head?

Caught in the flashlight's glare,
she pauses momentarily in the grass.
I want her body pooled softly
in my open palm;

I want to touch her life
the way a lover kneels in awe
before the mystery of another self,
a covenant with trust.

So much of living
is this grasp for nothingness
clothed in supple beauty:
it takes away my breath.

Dew-spangled and poised
on the ever-after's threshold,
I hear the insects trill
to each of us: let her go.

Elegy in a Snowstorm

I.

There are those who believe
a banyan tree links heaven to earth,

that angels slide off its patient limbs,
dream wanderers drifting down like water

from the helm of a radiant ship,
to mingle freely with women and men.

But I have seen the king cobra
untangle itself from the branches

to lie coiled and braceleted with dew,
its wide hood flared into a spoon

that wags back and forth and back,
stirring the air with death.

II.

Tonight the fertile jungles
are a secret chamber

housed in a vacant thought.
Where the bee prowled for pollen,

where bee-eaters perched on dahlias,
and peacocks wailed like widows,

there is only the tick of snow—
glittering, blowing, chill—

it disguises a garbage can as a nun;
it will inherit our shadows.

III.

The heart thickens like a storm.
You are gone for good,

and I have spent weeks, months
trying to know what it's like

to be dead.
The snow understands

nothing except itself:
a skull of ice, melting . . .

IV.

When you died, I felt
for the first time like a bride

left standing at the altar,
my shoes full of blood,

the small bones of my fingers
dazzled by pain, the bald rabbi

screaming Hebrew in my ear.
And your touch truly lost forever.

V.

You taught me how to dance.
We were sixteen then, and our bed rose

like a cloudbank or a rare carpet woven
right out of the Arabian Nights.

Soon we fell together into adulthood:
the heavens turned threadbare, strange.

And now you've fallen into ground,
where turbaned men in moustaches

kiss your golden lips closed,
as your spirit splashes itself with dust.

VI.

Alex, it has been snowing wildly
for more than a month.

It is sweltering in the house.
My breath is a kind of wake,

my sighs immense and empty.
Is the dark a doorway? Or the light?

I would hold you in my arms, here,
in this Valley-of-Bewildered-Windows,

if only you would slide back down
the long, white branch of your going,

and astonish us with your voice.

—in memory of Alex Londres, 1950–1988

Meditation at Twilight

Near a small village, not far from Bangalore,
I saw a king cobra flattened by a truck
and left to fatten the rush of red ants.

A baby cobra slid out from the wayside grasses.
It ran its delicate body up and down the corpse,
as if trying to coax it back to life.

All the world seemed stilled upon its axis.
Even the cicadas held their wings
in suspended animation.

Dust settled like a void.

Like a prism, each life reflects itself
in the dew's microscopic mirrors.

Every death records the silence
of a single, astonished mourner.

Bangalore Lullaby

The house is dark,
the mats laid out upon
the moat-like floor;
a scent of *ratri-rani*
floats upon the air,
and all the world's
enfolded into sleep,
or into earth's repair.

How vaguely stars
scout out the night
that hoods the city
in a grief of clouds;
how dimly glows the
moon's curved wick,
its lamp unit,
yet pooled in oil.

Now, only lovers stir
beneath a wavering sky.
Each turns to each
with golden cries,
their mortal bodies
rising up then falling
back into a shrine
of tangled hair.

So love illumines us
like windows sprung
by swarms of fireflies;
and each soul's light

briefly flickers on and
off until the darkened self
rises aloft the stairways
of night, and disappears.

A Brief History of Punctuation

*"No iron can pierce the heart with such force
as a period put just at the right place."*

—Isaac Babel

*"Cut out all these exclamation points. An exclamation
point is like laughing at your own joke."*

—F. Scott Fitzgerald

"Commas, like nuns, often travel in pairs."

—Mary Norris

A BRIEF HISTORY OF PUNCTUATION

I. The Creation of the
Question Mark

It grew slowly, atom by atom, curving
its serpentine line around a doubt.
For eons it hung suspended in the air
like a shepherd's crook, an ebony cane
a blind woman hung out at midnight
on an invisible clothesline.

It did not form itself from Adam's mouth,
it did not sprout as a kinky white hair
from Gilgamesh's never-trimmed beard,
it did not electrify loose ganglia
into syntactic fright in God's mind,
nor curdle the earthworm, nor shape
the sickle that mows down everything.

Like a lily, it roused itself to life,
unfurling into reason's limbo quietly,
and it left in its wake a single teardrop,
a tiny pinprick of dew, a dab of salt
for the minions of air to lick eternally—
that minute mirror begetting wonder.

II. Ellipses

. . . mark the passage of time through
a tunnel with no exits nor windows

. . . mimic Hansel and Gretel's bread crumbs

. . . imply that the massacre of the innocents
has been replaced by empty white trousers

. . . struggle to find, in the lie, the diamond sutra

. . . reveal the forty ruined catacombs and
copper altars destroyed by the last war

. . . are beloved of stone skimmers

. . . fuse the sad story of the Girl with Brass
Teeth with the tale of the Play-Doh Effigy

. . . because everyone has three open secrets

. . . which lead to the pause in the senator's speech
before he publicly confesses

. . . following the loud nuptial toast, during which
the bride's womb trembles with a tiny heartbeat

. . . opens the lips to receive a kiss

. . . and from the ruptured piñata
an avalanche of demons spills forth

. . . but there was no denying that

. . . and who to ask? From whom
to demand genuine sorrow?

III. The Inception of the Colon

Once while wandering across a field pulsating
with thousands of red poppies, the juggler

stopped midstep to consider the general and
undeniable beauty of the world. It was April,

and the breeze-ruffled, pollen-laden air
dizzied his senses. He pulled two acorns

from his pocket and tossed them up into the ether.
The green one equals my mother, he said,

and the brown one equals my father: yin and yang:
male and female: heart and mind: fork and spoon:

life and death: sky and earth: day and night:
this and that: verb and noun: beginning and end.

And when he caught them, many years later
while standing over his parents' rainy graves,

he again tossed them up into the ether, saying,
skull and seed: son and daughter: truth and lie:

water and fire: salt and sugar: tooth and nail:
thumb and pinkie: oil and vinegar: yes and no:

lovers and strangers: body and soul—then
the juggler saw that the acorns had turned

into two weightless words whose meanings
he couldn't fathom, and now those two words

shrank within his palm into: the fang marks
of a viper's bite: the coins laid yesterday

upon his mother's eyelids: the hair-wreathed
nipples stiffening under his sodden shirt:

the birthmarks on his enemy's knee: the disks
of moonlight touching his earlobes. And so

the juggler lay down upon the wet ground
next to his own loneliness, overwhelmed now

by the opiate fragrance of fielded poppies,
by their ruby-tongued furor, their ravishing

redness, their festive pyre from which arose
the palest motes of two ashes: twin ghosts.

IV. The Era of the Period

It was a civilizing urge—
to bring closure, to come full circle,
to worship time by divvying it out
into portions, increments, sentences.

All things must end, mustn't they?
Breath, as well as mortgages, as well
as prison terms, marriage vows, etc.
It was a civilizing urge—to end

one thought and begin another,
to pardon a slight, borrow a rake,
castle the future, crib the past,
count each day, siphon the moment.

But what about *before* this era,
when the currents of time flowed on
eternally through our veins through
our minds our souls our lives when

all bodies were charged by turning stars
by the bisons' migrations the gazelles'
leaping the clouds' turmoil and the ants'
gyrations—the whole heaving universe

endlessly dancing? A civilized urge.
Necessary. No doubt. The way. Modern
minds. Work. Bidding the forbidden. To
halt. What else could we do? Period.

V. The Invention of the Comma

Even after the youngest colors had faded,
she was still in a coma, though no one had
ever witnessed such a long, solemn sleep
stretching beyond the weeks of prayers
and dire rituals the last shaman concocted,
beyond even soot stains from the Great Fire.

Thirty full moons crossed the deep heavens,
and her pinched body, curled in upon itself,
flowered slowly into a woman's, though she
ate nothing, though her sisters' deft charms
stirred no life from her flesh and no sounds
from her pale lips, yet her pulse drummed on.

It hurt them all to see she was lost to them;
thus, one starless night the elders encircled her
mossy pallet, crying out to their spirits, for
they could no longer bear the terrifying shadow,
huge and black, her slumber cast over them.
They'd pierce an elk horn through her heart.

But when Gray Tooth lifted the antler high
above his head, the girls and fathers weeping,
the boys clinging to their mothers, a wave
rippled the sleeper's brow—a delicate tremor
undulating down her cheek, along her jaw—
and a teardrop slid from the edge of her eye,

trailing a glittering comma through their lives,
causing an owl's *who?* to break that silence,

and the elk dagger to drop like an exhalation,
and the girl's trembling body to unfurl into
the interrupted moment, her eyes fluttering
open, that tear etched forever in our world.

VI. Parentheses: A Bestiary

The perfect plié
A scythe smiling sideways to itself in the mirror
The cowled embrace truth briefly endures
Two hands upholding an invisible melon
Tandem heels of bread
A way of drawing shadows into light
The (visible) witness who speaks *sotto voce*
The jawbones' cradle for a mute tongue
Twin hemispheres of gladness
The crescent moon wooing its perfection from a dark pond
Two arms encircling longing
A circle cleaved by white noise
The mind's innocuous radar
A mini-corral of neighing vowels
What the hips know
Cloned sickles facing off
The sentence keeping abreast of antimatter
Elliptical thought, luminous hangover
Small talk
A still cove nestled among archipelagos
What's kept within the Stetson's rims
A moat for transcendence
Icons to the dependent clause
Cryptograms to God
How not to confront the awesome head-on
Smoky hoops halved by fire
The dual haunt of archers
An interrupted yawn
Thin keepers of protocol
Mellowed brackets

Curtains drawn at mid-afternoon
Bent boughs that brake for small animals
What the ears balance between hearing and silence
A dovecote for cooing
Someone's aside in an elevator
Little sisters of the blind
The quays at either end of Half Moon Bay
Adam's ribs curved around the hole in the world's heart.

VII. A Hyphenated Rondo

Let's join hands, you and I—
my id married to your ego,
your bipolar mood swings latched
onto my subequatorial desires—

let's dance around the edge
of our *fin-de-siècle* blues—
shake-rattle-and-rolling our eyes
in high-energy, all-natural joy—

oh, let's (presto-*voilà!*) fly
in our full-sized V-neck T-shirts
into the air-conditioned night
like top-of-the-line paper kites—

let's boogie until the stars un-
do themselves like cutouts from
this zillion-year-old universe—
let's press our custom-fit mouths

together (be old-fashioned!) and
ride each other's merry-go-round
until our mortise-and-tenon joints
crack—yes, let's hyphenate our-

selves so that we're ever joined
at hip-and-rib-and-back-and-neck,
a wondrous Pushmi-Pullyu—
a tandem Jekyll-and-Hyde duet.

VIII. The Birth of Dashes

Flying islands were once common
at the beginning of the world—

they flew at a leisurely speed
above the burgeoning volcanoes—

and so, too, flying saucers, as flat
as black LPs and marked with spirals

concentrically: thus they echoed
the whirlpool, the sunflower's maze

of swirling seeds, and the cosmos
with its slowly gyrating stars.

And at the beginning—which fed
itself mightily upon the end—

people could levitate whenever
danger harkened, or when they fell

in love—the sweet touch of wind's
fingers massaging their backs—

and they knew that their shadows,
cast back to earth, resembled slate slabs

being dragged along the oozing peat,
and they wept to see such gravity.

Back at the beginning of time—
which came on as a postpartum

depression, long after the world's birth,
but long before words—things which

floated, sailed, or swooshed by, and
people who hovered, became scarce.

And God—who made a ceremony out
of everything, whose tongue was

longer than a flying carpet, and
who knew that language, sooner or

later, would enter people's minds to
seduce them into thinking about Him—

well, God decided to stretch out
a hive of beeswax between His hands,

pulling it east to west and around
the equator, like a long thought,

and fragments of this He inserted
quietly into people's minds, so that

ever since—oh, it's been forever—
we have interrupted ourselves with

that euphoric dream of suspending
our heavy lives in the honeyed lapses

strung tautly between the termini
of sanctity and forgetfulness.

IX. Claiming the Apostrophe

Was it the keen Serpent who first saw how
Possessiveness could snare people's hearts,
Making their fingers close like vises around
A perfect apple, or their lovers' wrists?

No, it was Eve, I think, who first witnessed
How loss gives rise to greed—who saw that
The fruit she offered Adam bore her mouth's
Perfect teeth marks, a cage of apostrophes.

We all know the story: how her gift became
A fateful deed, an eviction notice; how hers
Became *his* and begot *theirs*, launching them
Into sin, and marrying them to divisiveness.

Their fall from grace also wed love to death,
And gave rise to a sob welling in their throats,
A brandishing of air that ushered in a sorrow
Which would forever join and separate them—

Eve's birth pains; Adam's lost Eden; Abel's heart;
Cain's knife—and all bearing God's thumbprint.
So, the world became apostrophized: the tear's
Drop, blood's spangle on the brow: *ours* now.

X. The Semicolon: A Totem

Like a sperm forever frozen in its yearning toward an ovum,
    like a tadpole swimming upstream to rouse the moon's dropped coin,

like an ooze of oil spilt from an inky bubble, the semicolon
    signifies both motion and stillness, an undulant pause, a moment's
        stalled momentum.

It must have arisen from some toiling mind concocting a serpentine idea,
    one thought hinged to another, a startled gasp between exhalations;

it must have emerged like a comet's long tail from behind the hulk of thought,
    Isadora's scarf trailing her neck, before being pulled taut.

Surely it gives us pause, gathering up strength as it coils its diamonds;
    it waits for our minds to waiver and assemble, while it rattles bright-

toothed seductions; it swells to fullness in fractions of important breath—
    then strikes out silently, aimed at the heart of meaning,
        its venom art.

Ghost Orchid

"*If God lived on earth,*
people would break His windows."

—Yiddish proverb

The Ravens

Magisterial in pitch-blackened suits, loud envoys
From the realm of the dead, the ravens are gone.
All autumn the dusks have been cured of their cries.

Instead, the chimney smoke curls into small fists,
And blue jays, woozy with newfound dominions of air,
Flaunt their own pantomime of arrivals or departures.

Why have the ravens left town like a feathered exodus
Of the collective spirit? Conflagrations of dark flames
Singe my dreams nightly, giving shape to absence,

Yet I have seen where they have flown en masse—
Thousands gather like bats around Thunder Mountain,
Tattering its timberline, the sky wild with wings.

And it is You they meet there, surely, for why else
Their throngs whirling, dipping, soaring like omens,
Their bodies obsidian flints striking softly against

Heaven's resonant silence, their dark-bird voices
Ancient with longing, tangled and blunt, so human?
Like Moses, I have climbed that holy mountain,

And I have watched the ravens weight vast currents
Of air with resurrected cries, but still I'm blind
To their purpose and feel alone, diminished.

And like Elijah restored to earth, I have known
Another world, but I cannot name it nor return there.
Why give to ravens what You withhold from me?

What is this drama of roaring wing-beats You ignite?
Your divinity divides the world. You are a shadow,
Massive and billowing, more secretive than death.

The Search

I'm sick of celestial whodunits, wherein God
multiplies Himself like the eyes of a fly,

and blows another version of redemption
into the golden pores of the sunflower,

and inflates the tulip's mansion with ghosts.
Rubied maple leaves bloody the ground

with tattered clues to the afterlife;
acorns concern themselves, like plump nuns,

with the sacraments of summer that worms
sequester as holy grails. I have lost my way.

I'm weary of the world of deeds and men—
oh world of ten thousand leavings and losses.

The Great Sleuth of meaning divides Himself
too thinly for comfort and dwells alone

in this patchwork universe, surveying our sins
of omission, the falling stars His hot tears—

and love's the only grace binding us
to each other with invisible threads.

Where does my wandering take me, but
down into the deepest pit of bewilderment,

where my own death stares back at me,
unadorned, unforgiven, unknown?

The only mystery that counts is the one
I cannot solve. Such is my burden, my hope.

The Fallen Angel

One more tithe to the altar of seductions:
a rose tattoo on her rotund rump, and for that
she's lifted her dress, tucks a round of bills
into her sequined G-string, her lips pursed.
As she bends down to unfasten her garter,
the golden clump of hairs on her pubis points
its damp goatee to a breathless audience—
singed, the balding insurance salesman,
scalded, the Vietnam vet amputee wringing
his empty sleeve like it's the enemy's throat,
stricken, the barmaid who's seen it all before,
but who's in love with the star of Pussy Galore.
Haloed by cigarette smoke, the stripper moves now
as if traversing a slow dream—her blue dress
a silken sheen, a diaphanous mist thinly clinging
to her body—reptilian, sultry, she pulls her palms
and silvered fingers around her swollen breasts;
she sways to the silent baying of the hounds,
to the groundswell of heartbeats and tambourines;
she shimmies her cobalt hem waistward, and now
she ploughs her hands down until her fingertips
touch and tender that dew-spangled curl of flesh—
and she is moaning softly now, her violet eyes shut,
her throat tilted back like a flask of champagne
ready to exhale its evanescent song, her lips
swollen open, a mirror image to her flushed sex:
she is taken up in ecstasy, her spine arching back—
as if by invisible wings she's being drawn away
from the heaving men, their minds aflame, burning
like molten coils, their desire the oil-rich fuel
igniting her return to God.

The Rapture

There is a kind of celestial music
That crushes the heart rather than
Raising it aloft in buoyant prayer.
Its melody is so drunk and swollen
By bittersweet rapture that the heart
Becomes engorged and finally bursts.
Thus saints die from such a surfeit
Of divine psalmody, their hearts
Finally knuckling under the blazing
Of His tightly clenched fist.

Black Haloes

How does God hold up heaven?
We who wear His curse like a plague,
We who have fallen five hundred fathoms
Below His grace, who cringe like curs
Offered scraps by thieves—it is we
Who balance His scaffolds, who upraise
Our aching arms eternally to bear up
The golden planks and invisible girders,
Who balance huge cloudbanks on our heads,
Who hold up His gilt rafters and ceilings.

He has marked us well so none mistake us:
Though winged, we remain flightless,
Though immortal, we yearn for a reprieve,
Though comely, we're repugnant to others,
Though undamned, we exist among flames.
Black haloes are suspended above our heads:
Our rings of gold tarnished over with grit.
Our only misdemeanor: a mineral existence
Troubled by doubt, disbelief, defiance.

Still, we were good men and women.
We believed. We gave alms to the poor;
We made ourselves gardens of pure deeds.
We sang canticles of love in His name.
Now, even the vultures snicker at us
As they flap past like the devil's wind.
Was it a sin to laugh at His solemnity?
Did our misgiving habits of flesh and mind
Postpone our access to heavenly pleasures?

Why can't God hold up heaven without us?
Our haloes slip and tilt, sag like doilies.
We suffer great pangs of yearning, despite
His lofty provisions of rosy forgiveness.
Holy outcasts, chastened zeros—we hum
Our harmonium's chord, pitched high above
Limbo, but we remain grace-haunted, stilted,
Lashed like vines to the pillars of paradise:
Forever upholding this Kingdom of Sighs.

All Souls' Day

I ask you, Is your soul still open?
Does the sound of Gabriel's trumpet
Install in you the glory of God?

I am a weak creature: I find fault
With the universe and its creator,
Whom—or whatever—that may be—

And there are days when I'm undone
By a nameless grief, by my marrow
Singing only to itself for alms.

And there are weeks when love
Appears to me—in the form of a dog—
And I can no longer bear to call it.

So, I ask you, Where does it dwell,
This thing called soul, this mirage
I feel pricking my nerves with gall,

This clear shadow made manifest only
By doubt and doubt's sister, trouble,
Or by doubt's beleaguered bride, faith?

I have waited, like a saint, alone
On the Bridge to Nowhere, and I swear
To all that is unholy and sacred:

My soul, my perplexed spirit, keeps
Its vigil all night, awaiting a sign,
Like a ship that can never dock.

Angels

Who are without mercy,
Who confide in trumpet flowers,
Who carry loose change in their pockets,
Who dress in black velvet,
Who wince and fidget like bats,
Who balance their haloes on hat racks,
Who watch reruns of famine,
Who powder their noses with pollen,
Who laugh and unleash earthquakes,
Who sidle in and out of our dreams
Like magicians or childhood friends,
Who practice their smiles like pirates,
Who exercise by walking to Zion,
Who live on the edge of doubt,
Who cause vertigo but ease migraines,
Who weep milky tears when troubled,
Whose night sweats engender the plague,
Who pinion their arms to chandeliers,
Who speak in riddles and slant rhymes,
Who love the weak and foolhardy,
Who hunger for unripe persimmons,
Who scavenge the fields for lost souls,
Who hover near lighthouses,
Who pray at railroad crossings,
Who supervise the study of rainbows,
Who cannot blush but try,
Who curl their hair with corkscrews,
Who honeymoon with Orion,
Who are not wise but pure,
Who behave with impious propriety,
Who hourly scour our faces with hope,

Whose own faces glow like radium—
Angels, whom we've created in our own form,
Who are without mercy, you seek and yearn
To return us like fossilized roses
To the wholeness of our original bloom.

Unfinished Psalm

I like how the days crescendo into night,
how the dark forms a rosary of hours,
and the full moon's the soul's white pendant.

Each dawn's an anthem for someone's deliverance—
not mine—for I'm still anchored to longing
like a nautilus to its spiraling house,

and only the tides of desire unloosen my hold.
December. The year dies anew, and yet
high clouds bear witness to change as they drift

into each other, reforming themselves sweetly
into origami cranes, rabbits, and doves.
Night's sum of shadows exacts my dues,

but whom to pay? The darkness offers only this
temporary, shallow solace—a quiet place—
and it says, Who are you, oh voiceless one?

An Unkempt Brilliance I Fear but Cannot Name

The darkness around us is deep.
—William Stafford

I cannot curse God any longer—
my tears, the tiny apostrophes of loss,
splash onto silence, evaporate at last.

> *Is eternity a trove that harbors*
> *Only the mystery of our days,*
> *Without the torment of our nights?*

I will try to speak softly, wrapped
in my chains, my voice a current
of praise spangled with awe's pollen.

> *Why does the soul root itself in air?*
> *How does it climb out from spiraling stairs*
> *Of iridescent stars constellating the brain?*

Happiness is both precarious and ancient.
Like Solomon, I sit on a makeshift throne
that wobbles when I lean toward one extreme.

> *And why shouldn't the soul be incestuous,*
> *Loving sister and brother, mother and father,*
> *Without the harnesses of guilt, remorse, shame?*

God, both pistil and stamen, beckons to me,
honey-suckler that I am: but when I slip
my tongue into irises, tulips, I sip only air.

The body, blood and muscle, muddles the mind.
The mind, fisted around ideas, bristles the soul.
Does the soul half-remember these coils?

After a death, my forebears sat shiva:
on small wooden stools they fasted, prayed.
Did God finger their cheeks with tenderness?

Yes, life's mosaic is clarified by dust,
The way a handkerchief covering a corpse's face
Blanks out the tragic jowls, the obstinate stare.

If I curse now, let me grit my teeth
over my exile from sanctity, which,
like alum turns the tongue fugitive.

The body can only take so much rapture.
The throaty fugues of pleasure dwindle,
Surely, to a final grace-note of molecule.

Dampness settles in my heart and art—
the wash of memory blurring my questions.
There are no hard edges to the Unknown.

I think the soul must be God's template,
Or templet ("miniature temple"), that place,
Like the stanza, encompassing strange music.

How have I slipped so easily from blame
to reverence, from hurling stray stones,
to blessing my wounds, startling as garnets?

Does the soul grow in increments of grace?
Does it move from one body to the next,
Receiving a rent of purest light from each?

I am still a child dressed in wonder.
But I am naked, too, under a nightgown
of clouds, under the shroud of my name.

Is the clatter of bones God's tambourine?
No, no—it can't be that a human thing
Yields music to ghosts—or can it?

Slight are my vows, cool my promises;
my unspent devotions are slippery as eels:
there is an unkempt brilliance I fear.

If love is eternal, then why not desire?
Its fire also pulverizes and scours,
Purifies—but perhaps that's a trick of light.

I still think that beauty is a blueprint
of the sacred. So, why not pain, why not
the broken mouth, and the hate it spews?

Why shouldn't the soul shake itself
Free of us, like a dog exiting water?
Our mortal smell, alone, must make it gasp.

But I feel something clinging to my flesh,
burnishing it in slow degrees like a patina
or a rash: the touch of God-knows-what.

Is the undertow of an echo a random shifting
Of a spirit's breath, or is it merely wind
Chimed and slimmed by flight from paradise?

I'm done with curses, done with clotted anger,
though they've led me, a churchless penitent,
to this threshold of God-hobbled astonishment.

Transubstantiation

First the high road, then a bend
in the river. Soon, a crossing, the sound
of waves, and finally, a clearing:

like a dragon's mouth, Galilee glistens,
white caps for teeth; a tongue of sunlight
streaks across the fiery blue—

Here the beleaguered come: the lame,
the amputees, the fly-covered misfits;
wan pilgrims pitched onto weeping shores.

And golden is he who steps out daily
from the dark rooms of shadow—
the man whom stray dogs feverishly guard,

he who can summon the stars at noon,
who blinks throngs of wasps into flight,
who makes the dun stones speak before

they blossom into bread, who comforts
the dying, passing his fingertips over
their lips as lightly as a kiss.

And there is an arc of strangeness
about his form, as if a black swan
invisibly cradles his shoulder blades—

as if the soft machines of air
erase his breath with plumes of scent
culled from the cedars of Lebanon—

And he is as a temple before them.
No birds sing in his presence, nor dreams
visit the children humming like locusts.

There are the pangs of love suffered
even by shoals of fish the outcasts net
from the water's pastures; the scarlet

and black gifts of tongues that vultures
offer as their worship; the little live things
that women bring: all ceremonies of devotion.

The sound of quarreling waves quiets when
he passes, and the wide maw of horizon
turns fangless and silken, tamed by love.

He is no prophet, but simply a man
chosen by the lion, shaped by exile,
a measure of music traveling deserts,

a singed offering, a white sparrow,
a fugitive sorrow, a flask of spring snow,
a user's manual of the spirit—

and you will know him when he arrives
without fanfare, without hosannas,
for the face he wears is your own.

Benediction

Bless the man with the torturer's mouth,
bless the woman with the fossil soul,

bless the man with the storm in his groin,
bless the woman whom no one loves,

bless the man with a skull made of iron,
bless the woman who dreams of great kingdoms,

bless the man who's strange and swift to anger,
bless the woman whose habit is silence,

bless the man who surrenders nothing,
bless the woman who's a martyr to pigeons,

bless the man who lurks in the tower,
bless the woman of no conscience, no armor,

bless the man who nightly cries "Wolf,"
bless the woman who blushes and stutters,

bless the man who subdues the trees,
bless the woman who curses the rainbow,

bless the man who is a slave to pity,
bless the woman who delights in nakedness,

bless the man who is broken by love,
bless the woman who heals herself in greed,

bless the man whose grip is slipping,
bless the woman who is dangerous with pride,

bless the man on the threshold of jumping,
bless the woman newly born into pain,

bless the man be he murderer or thief,
bless the woman drooling in her cup,

bless the man with a worm for a tongue,
bless the woman with a shadow for a heart,

bless the man who forgives only himself,
bless the woman who shoulders the world,

bless them all who are nameless and mad,
oh bless the man, yes, bless the woman.

WEAVERS

*Fifteen ekphrastic poems based on the
eponymous paintings by Baila Goldenthal*

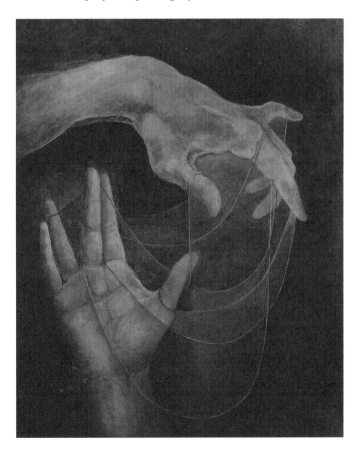

No. 4 in *Cat's Cradle Series*, Baila Goldenthal, 1995. Oil on wood panel, 18.5" x 15".

I. Sisters

The flaxen slipknots unravel in rivulets,
as if some strange alchemy persuades them.

One sister reigns them in; the other, kneeling,
her voice stained by sleep, sings in the shadows.

The elder wears her rose batiste loosely,
like an angel's smock spun by satin moths;

the younger's sheath's an arabesque of fire,
and her feet are clad in charcoal slippers.

Night is a balm, its carbon waves shot through
by the filaments of one girl's song, while

the other's reprimands scallop its dark edges.
How true the elder is to grief, which spools

her mind's thoughts upon its dim spindle,
that opens and closes her heart's portal.

She's not yet told her sister, who's joined
to her by arteries of twine, that the seines

they'll soon string upon the upright loom
are destined to enmesh the fabric of a pall.

The younger blindly sings so lightly for what
her fingertips divine: they are sweetly shaping

a swaddling cloth for the elder's unborn child.
Her touch is gossamer, her face obscured.

Such are the pangs of living in this world:
joy and sorrow each disguised by rote gesture—

joined by the casual, linked moment wherein
one sister blithely kneels to the other's torment.

"Sisters," No. 1 in *Weavers Series* (1990). Mixed media collage on canvas, 15" x 19".

II. The Wedding Dress

She hopes to banish anger like dust;
thus, the broad-browed mother's gaze
bends to meet her daughter's supplication:
she'll rescue the ribboned chaos from ruin.

A geometric light, sulphurous and spare,
ignites the daughter's undowsed pride—
her fury calmed for the sake of love,
though trust's betrayal dims their lives.

Her mother wears the teal tunic they wove
together years before, when her father
charged all their rooms with ghostly music,
and a web of light frilled every surface.

The father's absence is a stillness,
parenthetical, yet hovering between them
like a smoking lamp's blackened wick,
as they restring the heddle and the quill.

How cruel all separation is, the girl thinks,
for death's touch coats the threads like wax.
Yet her mother's fingertips are sure and deft,
thumb and digit reviving their silent minuet.

Often the daughter's dreamt this bridal gown:
smooth as a gull's breast, its waist cinched
like a wasp's, its hem aswirl in white roses.
That dream soothes her now, as does a flicker

of remembered breath, the honeyed aftertaste
ushered from her soon-to-be husband's lips;
it lifts her gray eyes upward again to face
her mother's taut-lipped frown, where anger

seems an embellishment of loss: so, each
sees her losses as frayings of the self,
then as reweavings of a delicate truce,
a consummation of both fear and hope.

"The Wedding Dress," No. 2 in *Weavers Series* (1990). Collage, oil on wood panel, 20" x 24".

III. Rapture

Who can say what has pricked their hearts,
blistered their minds until the room spins

like a carousel caught up in a tornado?
Some potent agent has flushed their skin

with heat, confused their graceful gestures
into a calligraphy of foreign phrases,

turned their tongues into clicking wheels,
their voices into blurred and husky echoes.

They feel seasick at first, the heavy clouds
pounding down on the roof, the room's walls

depressed from the wind's steady lashing,
the floor magnetizing the soles of their feet

so that they drown in their own gravity.
But then, suddenly, a clear-headedness

takes them up onto the shoulders of air,
lifts them like smoke, quickened, weightless,

and they pivot like angels on the head
of time, pilot themselves toward the rafters,

where, finger by finger, they burst through
the sky's threshold to the other side.

"Rapture," No. 3 in *Weavers Series* (1990). Collage, oil on wood panel, 20" x 16".

IV. Madrigal

Though it's late, and the house hushed,
they've arisen from their beds

to orchestrate the loom's revival,
to leash and knot two dozen strands

into a litany of angled lines:
two sisters working in silence,

their hair golden, their hands callused.
Outside, a quartet of crickets sings

and chides them, as if the insects
sense what they cannot: that night

is for untying day's desires,
for unlacing chance.

Though tired, they persist.
The younger girl, dressed in ochre,

remembers Leonardo's sketches,
all too vague and poorly scaled,

of a loom lifting mechanical arms
from either of its sides.

She smiles, content to turn
the oiled wheel above her, its spokes

radiating like oaken petals.
Her elder sister, clothed in red,

leans backwards, her arms' muscles
straining as she struggles

against sleep, against her urge
to turn away from their weaving

and the crickets' yearning.
To keep from slipping,

she's planted her smooth bare feet
firmly on the ground, so they

may make of their resolve
a tapestry as finely wrought

as pond water—warmed by the sun,
transparent—its sheen

as seamless as the only dream
from which the dead awaken.

"Madrigal," No. 4 in *Weavers Series* (1991). Oil on wood panel, 16" x 20".

V. The Virgin and the Widow

One figure hums a dirge, the other pulls
a song from her frame, its notes exploding
noiselessly into the room in waves of light.
But why must the cloud-clad woman lean
so far back into her strength,

while the other occupies her mourning
clothes with steadied ease, a firmness
rounding her shoulder, guiding her gaze?
Why must purity strain in white heat
against the cold verticals of night?

What grounds these women is a world
crimsoned by both birth and death,
that stepping-off place bloodied
by alternate acts of cruelty and love.
They must move together and against

each other, balancing their efforts
with strenuous care, sinewed touch,
so that the fibers they'll instruct
may enfold both newly born and corpse.
The dark one turns her spoked wheel,

while the breastbeam turns, unwinds
its angled line that leads the yarn
downward, past the solid battens
that could support a ceiling perhaps,
or a heaven neither wants nor forgets.

Their loom staffs their dance,
becomes both maypole and cross,
a post by which they station themselves
to the fierce or gentle motions of their art,
to the warp and weft of their hearts.

"The Virgin and the Widow," No. 5 in *Weavers Series* (1991). Oil and wax emulsion, 24" x 28".

VI. The House of Women

Each room's both oracle and tableau
vivant, wherein nine revenants reside
to play out each unperfected role:
there sits the mist-weaver, *bride*

of gloom, whose concave lap conceals
a cosmic void drowsing in her womb.
And there: *a girl perplexed*, who feels
she's flying a kite, and yet the room

is windowless, and the girl's spool
feeds out its line so hard and fast
it burns her fingertips raw.
Perhaps she knows that, next door,

death turns her own head upside-down
as if in adoration, as if in awe: for cornered
above her, and the house's other laborers,
sits a prioress of pulleys, *phantom queen*—

whose merest glance ignites their spirits,
whose body's nimbus siphons the light
from some star-drenched eternity,
threading its lengths of brightness

through room after unreeled room—
light stretched like silver turned
molten by the touch of every woman—
then cooled, looped, coiled, and cinched.

Among these revenants, only *the twins toil*
daily in their homespun gowns to coax
those shivering tapers into substance,
weaving a tapestry as weightless as evening.

Everyone indulges them, and why not?
These two are not yet frozen by a dread
of incompletion; they bend like rivers,
warmed by a fever of unknowing.

The *last three sisters* measure out
all the tenants' fates, entwined,
except for death's whose corner shroud
of light engulfs and clouds their minds.

The house's rooms hum an odd lullaby
as each person's tethers are unfurled.
The loom creaks and groans and sighs.
Nine women, one by one, restring the world.

"The House of Women," No. 6 in *Weavers Series* (1991). Mixed media on wood and canvas, 33.5" x 48".

VII. The Healer

This is true—we all know it for a fact:
life is full of ruptures, entanglements
of heart, bad brews and bad blood, gaps
between duty and desire, cruel calamities.

My friends, prophets and realists alike,
would counsel most to seize the day,
as if living from heartbeat to heartbeat
could seal our fate from error, or at least

numb us to a future that's tense,
to a past that's fragmentary as a ghost.
I say: within the moment dwell all moments
lived and unlived, all wounds and scars.

When I heal the gouged-out flesh, I heal
as well the broken will, the punctured heart,
the mind massacred by doubt, the self that
must stay sutured to the spirit, at all costs.

Like the fishermen who mend their nets daily,
so that dolphin and shark may swim freely
of their catch, so too do I mend only enough
of a person that cannot escape his own grasp.

For what is healing, if not our movement
toward being whole, and what is wholeness
but a way of becoming both wound and wounder,
the needle's open eye and its sharpened sting?

Sickness and health—both may or may not be
illusions: the secret is, know how *not* to die,
and learn that lesson in the midst of breathing,
then swim free of the lacunae in your mind.

"The Healer," No. 7 in *Weavers Series* (1991). Oil and wax emulsion on wood panel, 24" x 14".

VIII. The Saint

We are all charlatans of some kind,
donning vestments blue-black as bitter water,
putting on a blind life, a hood of false armor.

Today I'm a prophet, a changeling woman,
chaos stooped on one side, on the other, order;
both serve me as I play out my role of mother

of exiles, an unwed bride bestowing
small islands of the blessed with ardor.
Daily they come before me, as to a door

yawning open with hopeful light;
bowing low, their hems scrape the floor,
their faces apprenticed to a spell of glamour.

I tell them that grace resides only
in the folds of their unwitting grammar:
they must tell me their tales, one by one,

stammer out their awkward names,
places of birth, crimes and misdemeanors,
all the little lies that make them who they are.

But today at dawn, two arrived
who were mute, and grim as nightmares:
I knew they were envoys from another world.

All morning I gave them tasks
neither difficult nor lively: to reorder
a bushel of plums into a pyramid; to repair

the worn shoes of supplicants;
to scatter chia seeds to all the pensioners
drawn to my tree-lit, sun-doilied courtyard.

Now they ravel string around
my spools—Oh, it's a cruel power to watch
their clumsy, purposeful motions for hours.

But I grieve most for myself,
for I'm engulfed by a beauty more terrible
than their sobering realm across the river.

This beauty is the awful curse
from which I hide in good deeds, endeavors
so cleverly selfless, I fool even the weather.

See: I raise my right hand slowly
and water rains down for the famished farmer
dazed by years of drought; next, I murmur

and the crippled boy shouts—"Look,
I'm saved, I'm saved!" as he drunkenly whirls
round and round my industrious, silent watchers.

It's only a matter of time before
those thirsty two raise their patient fingers
to my face to pull away its fleshy torpor,

and expose the skeleton beneath:
my cheekbones sinewed by deep despair,
polished by fear; my marrow a sweet nectar

that they'll drink and drink,
   as if my virtue, sacrifice, and honor might
   restore them, once more, to the bruised world.

"The Saint," No. 8 in *Weavers Series* (1991). Oil and wax on wood, 24" x 14".

IX. Epiphany

It would be good to say
that we are sisters who have entered
into our characters the way a newborn
grows into his face, or the way music
floods a room until it trembles with sound.

It would be enough to know
that our tongues are shuttles moving
between day's recitals and night's torpor,
between known and unknown, just as purpose
and passion join hands in text and texture.

But the mirror flings us
back upon ourselves like water
splashed into a fire, and the steam
rising from our voices is doubt-charged.
We are seven strangers, not sisters;

we are fluid, not static
in our beauty, and our mirages
hover before us before deconstructing.
Whomever we are, it doesn't matter
whether we name what lies beyond

the stations of each self—
Still, it would be good to lose
our singularity the way each raindrop
steps down into the ocean's amphitheater,
joining its tiny timbre to a watery cosmos:

good to string our harp-like loom
with threads as sturdy as timber, and,
with our fourteen hands, to flitter through
its vertical shadows like airy songbirds,
to end at the beginning of wonder . . .

"Epiphany," No. 9 in *Weavers Series* (1991).
Oil and wax emulsion on wood panel, 29" x 24".

X. The Unfolding

Suspended in that hour when light surrenders
to dark, and dark cowers with its secrets,
four women gather to appraise their labors,
surveying the patchwork of their patient hours.

One woman's heavy with an unborn daughter
not yet unfolded from her amniotic cradle;
another, like a chrysalis who's just split
the facing of her velvet prison, peers out

shyly from her budding hood of yearning;
below her rests the pensive matriarch who
mourns the passing years like lost children
half-remembered, half-forgotten, yet loved,

always loved beyond every recognition—
and leaning toward them all stands she
who is ageless, a woman clothed in ether:
hope's shadow, molded from cloud and calyx.

Carefully, they unfold the bolt of heaven,
the silken freight of a lifetime's weaving.
They grasp the homespun borders as if milk
was spilling through their aching fingers,

while Death grins from her dusk-lit corner,
her own veil embroidered by black widows,
sequined with decay, appliquéd by dust—
she's both guest and intruder here, gloating

because she knows all mortal fabrics fray
then disintegrate, though each in her day
may have shone as though articulated solely
from the moon's spindle, skeins of starlight.

Now, quietly, tenderly, four weavers spread
open the sheer horizons of their cloth, sift
their purest thoughts through its rich cascade
of swells and valleys, its constellations.

They are unfolding their lives, this cloth
of torments and pleasures, as Death smiles
like a mirror's image dipped in acid, while
the air unfurls its gold, invisible design.

"The Unfolding," No. 10 in *Weavers Series* (1991). Acrylic on wood panel, 24" x 29".

XI. The Dreamer

When his mind is unfettered by cobwebs,
when night drifts in to the pewtered shadows,
when the world is a cavern unlocking its secrets,
when the tiny hammer of his heart slows its stammer,
when his body turns in its quarry to settle softly
like a pilgrim fallen into sleep's vast continent,
when the swivel door to the grave opens, then,
he begins to hear a harpist in the field of glass,
and a delirium of dreams draws back the curtain.

Now he is famous for no one but the soul;
now he rehearses the descent of man, wherein
time no longer blackmails desire, and his blood
darkens like oil, and his lies are beyond repair.
Like an extinguished planet, he radiates exiled light,
while his father and mother, so long dead, unbind him
slowly and begin to pull his limbs from their stupor.
He has joined them in an alabaster city underground;
he hears their marrow talking aloud to his.

Is this the afterlife, he wonders, a cold temple
of doom, where there's nothing to feel but the love
of God: a great, shining tooth in an empty mouth?
But no, he sees through his shuttered eyelids:
the dove with its claws, the terrible, torn gills
and gaping eye of the wailing fish, the blue bull
of oblivion—all premonitions of borrowed breath.
He is teetering on the edge of some threshold—
tongue-tied, he is becoming someone else—

"The Dreamer," No. 11 in *Weavers Series* (1991). Oil on wood panel, 24.5" x 32".

XII. The Magician

There is nothing funny about destiny:
the miraculous is woven into the mundane.
Whether or not you believe in fate's schemes,
they exist in the sixth dimension, awaiting
some sleight of hand or mind to defy reason.

I have, you see, a rendezvous with time
to keep, and she wears difficult disguises—
sometimes she's a blind girl searching for night,
who thinks day exaggerates itself, who chants:
"I have arms, I have feet, I even have eyes

in the back of my heart—I'm the wildest card
in the deck, the Queen of Spades." Forget her.
I like time best when she's caught in a mirror
of unspeakable desires, when she pretends to be
ripe with golden losses, but is merely oversexed.

I even admire time's handsome guise as a eunuch,
with his hand jobs and reversible head stuffed
with intrigues: he's a good lad, though he squeaks.
Perhaps, tomorrow, I'll turn him into a stallion.
Perhaps I'll turn the epochs into curtains of rain.

My power is a slow rapture, and, like that sailor
with his muscular grin, I say, "I yam what I yam,"
though I'm much more than the sum of my parts.
I make people laugh, though you see *I'm* not smiling.
This work is serious biz, this reworking of the real

into the sidereal, into a chorus of gasps and sighs.
My library's stocked with puns and punishments;
my calendar's loaded with impractical jokes—
I'm the captain of this ship of fools, a trickster.
And the wisest trick I play is on myself.

Come then, be light of heart, be merry, levitate
yourself above your covenant with dust—look
alive, entwine the fibers of your being with mine:
desire is the only fuel most of us ever require
to materialize blue angels out of thinnest air.

"The Magician," No. 12 in *Weavers Series* (1992). Oil on wood panel, 31" x 24".

XIII. The Outcast

I haven't always worn this telltale outer robe
made scarlet by the shame of others' secret tears.

No, long ago, years before I was washed up upon
a shore of corpses, before street urchins shunned me

like a rare contagion, a crimsoned crime enfleshed,
I stood among poplars in the city's careful gardens:

I grew tall among a firmament of smiling faces,
nurtured, honored by my peers, favored by the rich,

flushed only by good fortune, shaded by low arbors
latticed with the nodding glances of snapdragons.

That was another life. Now, I live on the outskirts
of the mind, where the towers stand empty, haunted

by raucous ravens, where a sprawl of graffitied stone
spells lewd epithets in a hundred foreign tongues.

Was it so terrible to live truly as myself?
I never harmed a single soul; I loved purely—

giving my body to my lovers, man or woman: a gift
that asked no return except joy's enfolding arms.

But then my city's elders condemned and exiled me;
they marked me, seared my androgynous palm:

branding fear's mask on my right hand. Weeks later,
an eye appeared on my left, unblinking, iris-blue

as eternity, all-seeing, and inwardly divining what
they can't bear to know: that my blood's poisoned

only by their hate, that the crown of thorns
they thrust on my head has become a lopsided halo—

They'd have me be an effigy of sin, a skeleton
uncloseted, a cruel warning frozen in red torment,

love's ridicule and desecration, a monument of ash;
but what they've made of me instead is a human pyre

within which burns hope's fiercest, unquenched fires—
for I'm a testament to a power greater than theirs.

"The Outcast" (aka "The Head, the Hand, and the Eye"), No. 13 in *Weavers Series* (1993).
Oil on wood panel, 14.5" x 6".

XIV. The Lover

The sky is a house of gilded mirrors set afire,
and I'd shatter them all, if I could, with song.

Yet I can't stand still: my bare feet sidestep
the day's shadows, my hips stir the moist currents.

My mind's aswim with a swarm of sultry fragrances
that the breezes peel and lift from my garden:

frangipani, lavender, sweet pea, and wildwood rose—
perfumes entangling me in a swoon of phantom petals.

And I'm trapped, too, in the beehive of my body:
when I move, I'm honey poured in slow motion—

sap's surge as it flows upward into green arms.
Suddenly a stillness claims me like a fever,

and I hum, a tuning fork struck by yearning.
I'll make of my waiting a ladder, a scaffold, a weir

of windows: Am I mad? Look! Something unsettles
the field beyond this golden haze—it's my love,

striding toward me through the high grasses.
Aroused, the cicadas rev up their motors;

golden orioles orchestrate an ovation;
the buttercups burst open—

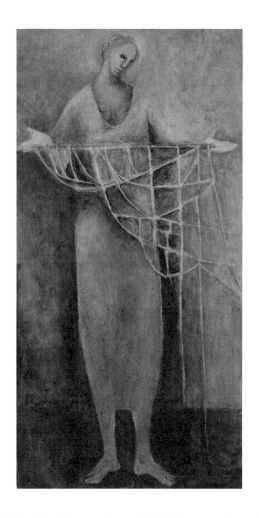

"The Lover," No. 14 in *Weavers Series* (1993). Oil on wood panel, 16" x 18".

XV. Benediction

What is this world but a long tapestry
of sighs interwoven every moment
anew, only to be undone, thread by thread,
at the loaming hour, in death's cradle?

May my painted words and wayward music
entwine brightly with your life, add color
to the blank canvas of your waking thoughts,
so that our minds merge with what's sublime,

otherworldly, beyond both tongue and touch—
so that the *spiritus mundi* washes over all
our senses, drowning us in a palpable light.
There is no god to whom I bow, but breath—

so, may my voice inspire vision in your eyes,
and kindle kindness in your fingertips that
bend to sacred or profane tasks and texts; thus,
we join every stitch in time to what's eternal.

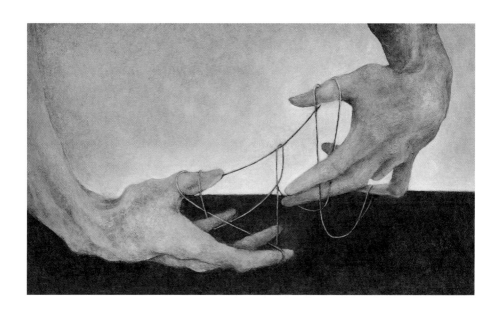

No. 3 in *Cat's Cradle Series*, (1995). Oil on wood panel, 12" x 20".

*"What would it mean to live
in a city whose people were changing
each other's despair into hope?—
You yourself must change it."*

—Adrienne Rich

Snow

For my mother-in-law, Margit Falk

1. Czechoslovakia

Blooming in your childhood in the thirties
there was a field so white in early June,
your grandmother said a frantic snow
must have fallen while you and Walter napped—
a miracle, she said, a celestial tablecloth
set with careful lace by Queen Anne herself.

Did you talk of Vienna with your blond playmates,
the local villagers, as you, your older sister, and
young brother, gathered jars of gooseberries for late tea?
Do you remember which children turned away
when the Nazis came, when the white field hardened
its mantle and your farmhouse went up in flames?

2. Vienna

The snow falls inside the glass dome.
It looks like dandruff, your brother jokes.
You have no mother to scold him, so you cuff
his shoulder, saying, "*Walter, Du bist verrückt!*"
The snow falls like logic from . . .
No, the snow swirls like memory—
The boy chimney sweep inside the dome
will lose his head.

3. Java

Three years, almost four, in the prison camp.
The jungle closing in, the Japanese guards
swollen with hate, with the yeast of fear,
with the humid swelter of the spiraling war.

In green canopies overhead, monkeys howling.
Army ants on the march. Maggots in the bread:
live snow, you think. Then you abandon religion
for a while. Then you pray.

4. New York

The Bronx delivers itself over to winter
like a novice taking the veil.
But the weather is blasphemous, wicked
in its relentless, futile devotions.
Why are you still alive?
Your mother, father, brother, sister,
brother-in-law, and nephew: all dead.

Bracing yourself against the sleet,
your belly grown round as a balloon,
you push on to the subway, your eyelashes
latticed with snowflakes, your footsteps
effaced, your breath exhaling ghosts.

5. Laguna Hills

Seizure World, your son calls it, this place
of palm-treed gentility, Southern California's oasis
for gray-haired denizens, for the Living.
From here you can see our Alps, fifty miles north,
where Mt. Baldy points toward a vacant heaven.

Some of your friends, survivors too, have moved out.
The locked gates, you say, disturbed them,
reminding them of the German camps . . .
But you like it here: the group bus tours
of Laughlin and Las Vegas, where you clutch
your purse in the great gambling halls,
suspicious of luck.

6. Mt. Baldy

Your eldest granddaughter bears your likeness
most: the green eyes, aquiline nose, sensual lips.
In college now, with a world history paper due,
she asks you about the war, and you weep.
A heavy silence darkens our Thanksgiving table.

Outside, snow-laden winds lash themselves
against the windows. The room stands still,
as if cupped in the eye of a tornado.
Then hailstones, tiny fists, awaken us.

7. Here

Some sorrows in this life bloom slowly
into the six-pointed stars of wisdom.
Others slow the blood or freeze it.
Some sorrows cannot salvage the soul
from a lifelong torment of nightmares.

Your shock of white hair is beautiful.
Beyond us, beyond the interior world,
the snow is as guileless as time or fate,
as it drifts down to frozen ground.
A light crossing your face dissolves

into tears, and those tears are mine,
too, though I do not choose them, just
as the beating heart, that brave and
vulnerable clock, does not choose when
or where or why it must stop.

.

Second Born

Dreamy daughter, how the room grows still
at last, dark seeping slowly out the sill.

Tiny veins climb the trellis of your throat,
and I watch your fingers, one by one, petal out

until your cry bursts forth, a trumpet blossom,
and every cell celebrates its new nation.

Now I feel myself falling back into place
as your grandmother scrubs from the sheets

the shadows of blood, and your aunt hears
with her fingertips your fluttering heart.

This time I felt death move through my limbs,
the whole room sinking into my pain,

and I thought the world too cruel for us both.
But here you are, and I am still afloat.

And how your awed face wonders about the light
touching the corners of my mouth. Tonight,

I hold you to my breast the only way I know:
as an arrow against my arm's bow.

Purview

Within this leaf mold, an ice crystal's balanced
        on the edge of melting into nothingness;

enclosed by the amniotic sac's enterprising cells,
        the salt of the oceans whirls and flows;

within the sleeping, granite mountainside,
        the silicates gather their shining tribes;

while all around us the fatal seasons move on
        from beauty to terror and back again

to the daily sessions of light and dark,
        even while my human heart, O assassin,

echoes such rhythms my human mind ignores:
        rain falling in fits and starts, then snow

flaking down the air's thinly traveled highways
        like so much cosmic dust, so much static.

On the butterfly's wings, a Rorschach smear
        of spring's delusions—no, only a shadow

playing against a frozen pane of window glass—
        the world outside mirrors the world inside,

a landscape I know but cannot touch . . .
        Only in that vast moment, when I surrender

my joy to the sorrow of living, do I know where
     I'm going, and why each breath returns me

like a pilgrim to the very beginning of self.

Dulce et Decorum Est

After Wilfred Owen

Bent double, like Atlas burdened by the world,
Bludgeoned, coughing up blood,
Rodney King succumbed,
Till on that graphic scene we turned our backs,
And toward our own rewards returned like ghosts.
We courted sleep, though wakeful, dazed, and lost
Amidst the limping decade shod in lame excuses;
Blind, drunk on media hype, and deaf
To our own consciences, we dropped our causes.

Gas! Fire! Quick boys—an ecstasy of fumbling,
Fitting stone to fist—turning the clock back,
But someone known was yelling out and stumbling
And raging like a man aflame inside.
Dim through the smoky screen and thick red light,
As through a nightmare, I see us drowning.

In all my dreams throughout the flagrant night
He plunges at us, swearing, choking, drowning.

If in some clarifying dream, you too could brace
The stanchions that were flung at him,
And watch the white eyes laughing in his face,
His broken face, human and sick of sin,
If you could hear, at every blow, the blood
Come gurgling from the fear-corrupted lungs
Bitter as the words,
The thoughtless wounds, festering guilty tongues—
My friends, you would tell with burning hearts
Your children ardent for some desperate worth, tell

Them the old truth: It is bitter and deadly wrong
To think each of us is *not* accountable for hell.

City of Angels

Night beyond our wooded deck is murderous.
Pandemonium erupts in static bursts:

the radio's high voices pitch themselves in waves
of terror through the nervous house, and we, adaze,

can only shake our heads in disbelief, certain
that before evening's curtain drops its tattered hem,

the city of angels will have fallen hellishly to ash,
each palm and signpost flaming like a giant, struck match.

Turn off the doom, I say, and soon the walls collapse
into solicitude; the air's held breath lapses

like a tide into the not-too-distant sound of water
gushing down from Angel Falls, and our younger daughter,

Leah, still awake at this raw hour, steps out
under the star-draped sky to look for what, I know not;

but there she stands, T-shirted cherub, lost in thought,
she who will inherit charred valleys, dumb forests, our doubt,

this clenched world, its lyres and lies, its comfortlessness.
Child, angel in darkness, living's both curse and blessedness,

and if I could, I would will a host of seraphim
to crowd around your head, to grace your every limb,

so that your passing though the harrowing, godless years
is lighted by others' tears turned inwardly to mirrors.

Bark with Authority

I tell my dog, bête noire of the backyard,
unbellicose beast, he with the musculature
of a canine warrior, all beef and brawn:
bark with Byzantine glory, with bravura;
bark with the rumblings of ruptured nerve;
be brazen and boisterous, be jowled in howls,
be loose in the lungs, a grounded leviathan;
be blue in the throat from sounding the alarm.
Rip your voice through the dazzle of the rich,
through the daze of the poor, through storm
and drought, through the whines of Boy Scouts
out on their hike, through coyote's whistle;
rouse your ruff to a roar that ripples
the air like a serrated knife, that riots
in the ear until the world shouts *Stop!*
But you, sad Sam, named for the word-man
who barked out a lexicon of rapturous sounds,
you with your doleful eyes, crooked smile,
with your quizzical gaze, your velvet snout:
you shrug your shoulders, tune me out,
would rather stand shyly behind sage Molly,
your surrogate dam, that grizzled old bitch
who's arthritic and wobbly, though still wily—
you'd rather yield to her dominance, yes?
Well, what's it to me if you'd prefer modesty,
being the foil, the sidekick, Laurel to Hardy?
What do I care if you live out your days,
indeed your dog days, without doggerel or dog-
eared memories, with a dogged suspicion, dog-
faced and dog-headed and -hearted, that you've
gone, doggone it, to the dogs, so to speak,

and that your only dogma, our only dog's letter
(trilled in your sleep when you're dog-tired)
that weathers your lips, begins with an "S"—
and ushers in snoozing and supper and silence?

El Día de los Muertos

Ten candied skulls are lined up ghoulishly
upon the shelves of La Boca Negra Bakery.

Though some stare gleefully at passersby,
others glare vacantly this All Saints' Day

into hot blasts of yeasty steam that waft
out like dreams from fiery ovens in the back.

Three whitened bakers exercise strong hands
to work doughy miracles in a careful dance

with time—The dead are all around us here,
and everywhere, though we are blind as air

and only feel their earnest gaze when knives
of loss peel back the stupor of our lives.

Hunger barely masks the longing in their eyes,
for they dine emptily upon our sighs,

yet hope to harvest sweetness from our breath:
the dead love us with tacit tenderness.

Behind the bakery, the Sunday mourners
picnic on the graves of family members.

Shivering in the cold, sucking the sugary bones
of their ancestors, expectant mothers intone

the names of their unborn, lives swelling like bread
leavened in the invisible arms of the dead.

The Dolphin

Just off the Santa Monica Pier,
a dolphin swam in tight circles
for hours, having lost its power
to echolocate a wiser course.

No matter that photographers,
marine biologists, and reporters
with their mini-cams and prayers
tried to will it from its torment:

the dolphin churned and turned
with dizzy ardor, as if devotion
to repetition could set it straight,
could help it navigate to freedom.

Was it toxins spewed in the ocean
that sent its brain to spinning,
or do dolphins, just like humans,
go off the deep end, either with

or without reason? Exhausted,
finally, the dolphin drowned.
On TV it looked as still as time.
But it keeps circling in my mind.

Waste Management

Every night a bear comes round our house to scare up
some windfall pears or to forage for fragrant garbage,
trudging on soft-padded feet & slightly open-mouthed.
He's an ursine Tony Soprano, I think, seeking refuge

from autumnal hungers as he forages the town's alleys.
Burly as a nightclub bouncer, near-sighted, he browses
through our lives' detritus, appearing as a refugee
from day's ample shadows. Our bear noisily chases

a neighborhood cat, a disemboweler of mouses,
then he eats the worst type of underworld scum—
larval worms in Day-Glo trousers—food storehoused
in a huge belly that sways to & fro when he travels.

Despite his slovenly slouch, our bear's a marvel
of Mafia etiquette as he curses & wantonly carouses
in the dim byways of the forest, as he sways in raveling air
to snap the bark off trees with his tough teeth & calluses.

We curse the furry rampages of our famished bear
who's surely gotten high on gruff power as he struggles
to grip trashcan rims with iron fingers—ever roused
to action by brisk whiffs of winter or our ribald catcalls.

O made man, living drunk or dour, don't settle
for trudging on soft-padded feet, staying tight-hearted—
know, as I do, how fear & desire drive us all. Look how
nightly a bear circumambulates our lives with such ardor.

A Small Elegy for a Big Dog

If there's a canine heaven, one lively
with gray but sprightly mongrels, crowded
with pedigreed hunters, crotch-nuzzling grunters,

with slender racers, splendid garbage surveyors,
with lonely, courageous strays; indeed, if there's
a heaven replete with every good pooch who

licked the proffered hand, chased the deft intruder,
towed the family sled, barked in throaty joy,
or howled despairingly from pain's depths—

then you, Sam, will have found your place among
a nation of loose-jowled, dew-clawed, crop-eared
brethren: the one-eyed Chihuahuas, mangy Shepherds,

the feeble vagrants, and teat-swinging gals, among all
the ragtag swimmers, leapers, scratchers, and grinners.
This is the least of what I wish for you, friend, now

that you're gone, when only a sole black hair left
on my trousers recalls your sleek, midnight coat,
your brown-eyed sweetness, your great soul.

May your heaven of dogs include one human
ghost, so that the lightest touch of her hand
leads you to a flealess sleep beyond all grief.

Marriage Vow

Contradiction is a lever of transcendence.
—Simone Weil

Does every choice constitute a loss?
Perhaps even the mild starlight
that swells our bed robs the night.

Our task is to choose our fates.
My father chose to become human
because he was born a god.

Your father scrubs away his father's blood.
Our mothers smear their thighs with soap,
hoping to purify themselves of birth.

As husband and wife our pact's with Eros.
Yearly we gather the still photographs
of our lives, making metaphors of desire.

I cannot save you, nor myself.
But listen: here is my life,
my pale heart, my baffling prayers—

here is the one you chose, whose name
burns a hole in your breath, whose love
tips the salt back into your tears.

Black Widow

This dangler who visits me
disguised as agile beauty
is death's sweet marionette,
an eight-legged, swollen speck—
a tiny, black forget-me-not
spinning her soundless tune
with a luminescent thread.

Her husband taps out a code
of courtship quite cautiously
as he slowly tightropes nearer:
pheromones prescribe his destiny,
yet he seems a wayward star
moving to collide into a sun
that will implode, unfurling
a million filaments of light.

I watch their dance tonight
and see extend through history
the sacrificial slant some lives
slide down upon—star, spider, man—
each body bright, marked for life
by an invisible hourglass that's
tipped, emptying its sand.

The Voyage

One night the barge from Yon to Hither
drew its silver wake across the river,

a sword splitting open a black serpent,
so that all the nets swelled into tents

taut with the bodies of a thousand fish.
Then from the darkened, unawakened south,

beekeepers arose from their waxen sleep,
as low bells summoned in the wayward sheep,

and the full moon capsized in the west,
bringing down the dark with its bayonets.

Wind rose to bicker with the red-eyed men
who smoked their cigars at starboard end,

who watched the stars blink off, one by one,
like distant windows in a distant town.

The barge rolled into a roar as we neared
the steepled hills, the walls, the busy pier.

Its slow, graceful body steered into open hands,
the ropes of daylight secure, night's passage

no more than a long scrawl of moonlight
written in our blood, an untranslatable quiet.

Ten Versions of Ruin and Repair

After Rumi

1

We break what holds us.
Still, powerful arms close around us.
Odd, this nervous greed for change.

And yet wise men will say both greed
and generosity are evidence of love.
Perhaps love is simply grief for the flesh.

2

The news we hear every night
is a kindling for the future.
What can anyone tell us that we didn't know?

Take this town with its open secrets,
its crowded gardens and dazed scorpions.
It's a place of noisy breathing.

For here, like anywhere else on earth,
even the thorns are mystically inclined:
every branch opens its arms to the universe.

3

I'm crying, so my tears tell my cheeks.
It seems there's this constant conversation
between heaven and hell, silence and speech.

Sometimes I'm ashamed of using words,
for the gold dish of the moon is more real
than the blue table I set it down upon.

Yet I see how lovely and strong
the meaning of each thing is.
Forget this life, I say to myself.

4

A girl runs barefoot through the house.
Outside, the white narcissus feeds on quiet,
while I sink to the bottom of my life

like a fish falling asleep in its tank.
Wake up! Stop making excuses.
It's time to grow a new tongue.

5

We've seen magicians levitate themselves,
from thin air materialize scarves,
handbags, bewildered rabbits.

Neither accidental, nor done with mirrors:
such intelligence is substance.
Indeed, Einstein knew this equation.

Surely, when we look for God,
God is in the look of our eyes.
Even the unfaithful wear this gaze.

6

What I can't understand is why
the dead long for what bruised them.
And why the living vote for politicians

who argue in favor of oblivion.
A pitcher shatters, the river meanders on.
We all yearn for the alchemy of verbs.

7

I am the seashell lying empty on the beach—
you are the water flowing toward it.
Not that I've done much to deserve the attention,

but, somehow, the stage has thus been set.
No mercy for the earthbound! So,
I'll love you even as you retreat from me.

But how is it you can breathe without a body?
And how can you interpret the sky so well?
There is only this one sigh between us.

8

When I see a woman's life torn
into a thousand pieces, or a man
whose face is a blackened stone,

or a child whose heart has been ransacked,
I know that when any one of us lets go
of our compassion, even for a single moment,

the world begins to collapse again.
Pain teaches us how destitute we are, how brief.
It is the mother of us all.

9

The world hurts me with its questions,
with its stupid and true answers.
What I need is a circle of wind,

a ring of thunder around me—
I need the kind of shining only
the ocean absorbs, and the stars.

10

There is a strange frenzy in my blood,
a red flurry, a rush of sparks.
Something invisible and dangerous moves

through me, from the soles of my feet
to the graying roots in my scalp.
Am I insane? Don't come near me.

Friend, for fifty years I've called out.
And for what? For this air? This poetry?
Gaze into my silence, cries the page.

And I listen.

The Raindrop's Gospel: The Trials
of St. Jerome & St. Paula

(a novel in verse)

*"It is a river of gold, a well stocked library,
that a man acquires who possesses
Jerome and nothing else."*

—Erasmus

"St. Jerome Adoring the Crucifix," Lorenzo Lotto, 1544. Oil on canvas, 20.8" x 16.5".

Genealogies

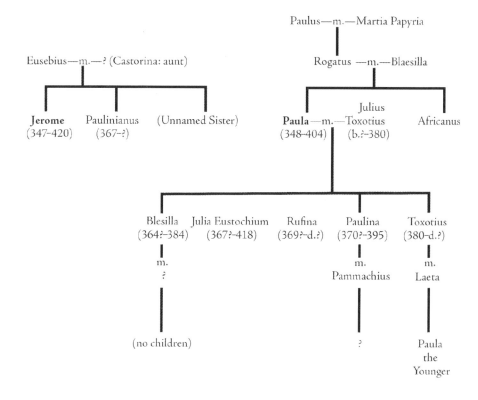

Paulus —m.— Martia Papyria

Eusebius —m.— ? (Castorina: aunt)

Rogatus —m.— Blaesilla

Jerome (347–420) Paulinianus (367–?) (Unnamed Sister)

Julius

Paula —m.— Toxotius Africanus
(348–404) (b.?–380)

Blesilla (364?–384) Julia Eustochium (367?–418) Rufina (369?–d.?) Paulina (370?–395) Toxotius (380–d.?)

m. ?

m. Pammachius

m. Laeta

(no children)

?

Paula the Younger

Chronologies of the Lives of St. Jerome and St. Paula

Circa 347 CE: Eusebius Hieronymus (aka Sophronius, later St. Jerome) was born in Stridon, Dalmatia, of affluent Christian parents. His father was also called Eusebius (Greek for "piety"). In his voluminous *Letters*, Jerome never refers to his parents, but he does refer to his brother Paulianus (Paulianian), to an unnamed sister, to his foster brother, Bonosus, and to his maternal aunt, Castorina.

359: At the age of twelve, Hieronymus is sent to Rome to study Latin grammar, rhetoric, and philosophy. There, during his adolescence, he becomes enamored of Latin literature, lives a hedonistic life, developing tastes for women and fine food, and often frequents the catacombs with his friend, Rufinus, who becomes his theological foe in later years.

366–372: In 366, Hieronymus is baptized and given the biblical name "Jerome," probably by Pope Liberius. He spends years traveling widely in Gaul, Dalmatia, and Italy, and staying in a variety of impermanent residences, while his attraction to monasticism, and to leading an ascetic life, grows.

373: Jerome begins a trip throughout the East but, due to fatigue and inner turmoil, he stops in Antioch in 374, where he's the guest of the priest Evagrius. It's here that Jerome composes his earliest work, *De septies percussa* ("Concerning Seven Beatings"). In 375 he suffers his famous dream in which he's dragged before God's tribunal, accused of being a Ciceronian, rather than a true Christian. He's brutally lashed in the dream, and he vows never again to own or read "pagan" (classical) literature.

374–377: Jerome spends three years as a hermit in the Syrian desert at Chalcis, searching for a confirmation of his faith and for inner peace. Here he suffers from loneliness, from stomach ailments, and from the temptations and passions of the flesh. His response to these trials and torments is incessant praying and fasting, the intensive study of Syriac, Greek, and Hebrew, the latter language taught to him by the (formerly Jewish) Christian convert, Baraninas, and his pursuit of a wide-ranging correspondence.

378: Jerome returns to Antioch, where he is known as an important scholar and monastic figure. Bishop Paulinus ordains him, accepting Jerome's condition that he not have to conduct any priestly duties, so he may return to his scholarly pursuits. During this time, he visits the Nazarenes (Jewish Christians) of Beroea to examine their copy of a Hebrew gospel (the Gospel of Matthew).

379–382: Jerome is ordained a presbyter in Antioch; he continues his scriptural studies, improves his Greek, and translates fourteen sermons on Old Testament books.

382–384: Jerome returns to Rome as Pope Damasus's secretary; he translates exegetical tracts and two sermons from the Song of Solomon. He also revises the Old Latin version of the Gospels, and holds classes for a group of noble Roman widows and virgins, including Paula and her daughters Eustochium and Blesilla. He teaches the group the Hebrew text of the Psalms, and serves as their spiritual guide and master. He later earns severe criticism from the Church for his questionable relationship with his female coterie, for his castigation of the Roman clergy and its lax monks, and for corrections to gospel texts. In 385, after Damasus's death, Jerome leaves "Babylon" (Rome) for the Holy Land.

385–389: Jerome leads Paula, her daughter Eustochium, and several other virgins and widows in a religious and archeological pilgrimage through Palestine and Egypt. In 386, he settles with Paula and Eustochium in Bethlehem where, by 389, he has used Paula's vast fortune to subsidize the establishment of a monastery for monks, a separate convent for nuns, and a library, built under Jerome's direction. Here he and Paula live, except for brief journeys, for the rest of their lives. His commentary on Ecclesiastes (c. 387) is the first original Latin commentary that relies fully on the Hebrew text.

392–393: Jerome completes *De viris illustribus* ("Concerning Illustrious Men"), opposing pagan pride in pagan culture, as well as writing the brilliant but often vulgar diatribe against the claim of equality between virginity and marriage. (Throughout his monastic life, Jerome suffers from lewd and lustful dreams.) He amasses a considerable library of important biblical texts and commentaries in several languages.

391–406: Jerome produces a Latin translation of the Old Testament (the Vulgate edition) based on the original text, a remarkable task. For his Vulgate translations, Jerome uses punctuation as a rhetorical system—*per cola et commata* ("by phrases")—relying on earlier texts by Cicero and Demosthenes. Thus, he becomes a pivotal figure in the development of punctuation.

420: Jerome dies on September 30 in Bethlehem and is buried beneath the Church of the Nativity, next to Paula's and near Eustochium's graves.

Notes

Medieval and Renaissance portraits of Jerome sometimes (anachronistically) represent him as a cardinal, and they often place him either in a monastic cave or in his monastery library, a lion lying at his feet, and several or all of these items nearby: a skull, inkwell, and hourglass. When he's not portrayed as a scholar and theologian, Jerome is often placed in a wilderness landscape and depicted holding a stone, a symbol of his voluntary asceticism and life of harsh penance. As St. Jerome, he serves as the patron saint of librarians and students.

Paula was born c. 348 and died at the age of fifty-six on January 26, 404. Most of what is known about her life is provided by Jerome's *Letters*, in which she figures prominently; however, her side of their correspondence has been lost. She was descended from two of the noblest Roman families of the era, the Scipios and the Gracchi. Paula was married to Toxotious and bore five children (four daughters and one son): Eustochium, Blesilla, Rufina, Paulina, and Toxotious. When she was thirty-two, her husband died, followed shortly by the death of her daughter, Blesilla. This period of extreme sorrow eventually led to her conversion to Christianity and to her lifelong association with Jerome. Rufina and Paulina were teenagers, and her son Toxotious only a few years old, when their mother, Paula, permanently left Rome for Bethlehem. After Paula's death, her daughter Eustochium assumed leadership of the convent founded by Paula and Jerome in Bethlehem; Eustochium's niece, also called Paula (the Younger), succeeded Eustochium as the head of this nunnery. Paula (the Elder) is considered the patron saint of widows.

Although I use historical facts detailed in various documents pertaining to their actual lives, I focus in this book primarily upon the relationship between Jerome and Paula, as I imagine it, rather than upon the former's religious commentary and treatises.

Though Jerome is often castigated by feminist theologians and medievalists for his diatribes against marriage and sexual passion—as well as for upholding virginity as the ultimate feminine ideal—I reveal him here as a character at war within himself, a man whose public persona and religious writing are in opposition to his private desires.

In several poems in this section, I refer to St. Jerome using his Greek name, Hieronymus ("devout"), during the earlier periods of his life.

M.S.

The Father of Punctuation

It is a river of gold, a well-stocked library,
that a man acquires who possesses
Jerome and nothing else.

—Erasmus

"St. Jerome in His Study," Albrecht Dürer (1514), engraving, 9.7" x 7.5".

Father of Punctuation

In moments between preoccupations, in those pauses
punctured by the sound of malm being ground up
by bricklayers, or by the scolding magpies, or by

Paula praying quietly with her garnet beads—
the click and suspirations—he swabs his brow and
thinks about what sets apart one interval from another:

how a specific point must be molded into significance;
how each phase of an Idea must be syncopated, or
rotated, isolated or expanded, until its complexity

rings as clear as brook water enshrined in a chalice.
And so he devises a system of symbols to serve as
toggles and bridles, pulleys and beams, sutures, store

houses, stopgaps, funnels, fonts, ferrules, pipe joints,
flasks, flashing, stoups, basins, hinges, splines,
lids, signposts, road markers, chain links, spindles,

faucets, footbridges, ducts, channels and frets, braces,
gears, mauls and gavels, girders and girdles, brackets,
clasps and gridirons, tiepins, torques and tourniquets.

But he must strive to make his symbols swift
and supple, like swallows' wings, economical in
stroke, uniform in use, non-ornamental, plain.

The marginalia of his pages bespeak his toil,
littered with the dashed off tokens, teardrop
shapes, cryptographic crescents, quaint codes

and puzzling ciphers of his mind's hieroglyphic
quest for shapely marks, some which signal when
to stop, where to pause, how one thought unites

another, or how it subdivides itself, or multiplies
its meaning, or terminates a ponderous question.
It takes him years to divine this system which

neatly supersedes Greek's network. How precisely
he lays out the deft marks—solidus, hyphen and punctus,
a doubled virgula suspensiva, ampersand, subscript,

vinculum, ivy-leafed hedera, parentheses, and last—
the philosophical, obscure economy of the ellipses.
He looks up from his fine labors: the night sky

blackly mirrors back to him the roiling galaxy
of quaking stars, fossil planets, the broadlit swath of
the Milky Way—all glowing ornaments of God's mind.

A Matriarch of Rome

A flinty afternoon stirred by a boost of breezes
brings back her other life—as distant now as the pouts
of her young daughters, as remote as the mercurial love
of her headstrong husband with his lapis amulets,
his stable of roan horses rippling with fervor . . .

Their days together rich, grandiose: cashmere shawls,
enameled flasks of sangria, strung emeralds crowding
her neck like beetles, marble walls and zebrawood tables,
the traffic of servants, raw fragrance of stacte, water's
clear slither, splash, and spill from myriad fountains.

She remembers their ebony bed's alcove, its criosphinx
mantle, the huge ram's head hewn from gray onyx;
she again stands by their window to gaze out on a city
scalded by summer gusts, the air thickened with grit
from the numismatists' shops, the nutmeg vendor
stalled under her eaves, hurtling oaths at a soldier.

All this, all this worldly commotion riots again
through her in painful explosions—a vision of Toxotius
stoking the coals, his muscled thighs auburn in firelight;
her palace herbarium fragrant with pressed petals;
taste of lichee and cherimoya, wisps of frangipani.

Winter nights she pored over her silver zodiac, plotted
her girls' betrothals by the stars' presage or turning.
In later years she was too often revived by passion—
the bloody spectacles at the coliseum, her yielding

to the intoxication of Remus's lips. Yes, it was true:
after Toxotius left her a widow, she coarsened.

Now the past's pageantry seems merely a paralysis
of will, or of faith, or both. Her life then, all idolatry,
indulgence, a plasma engulfing her in a brocade of sin.
All her protean wealth now nothing but dust and lint;
her husband, daughter—supine under the mimosa.

Paula (July 383 CE)

Paula's Tale: Mourning

In my thirty-third year, like our Savior,
  I was ripped apart by death, although I
myself did not die. A spring contagion seized
  my Silla's heart, bursting it asunder,

until nothing could bring her fitful
  laughter back; nothing could reverse
her quiescence, revivify her cold lips,
  nor rupture her lengthening silence.

I recalled the grinding of her teeth
  at night, her starling chatter over
breakfast, her noontime chiromancy
  lessons, her stable boy infatuations.

My Silla! How could you leave us
  here, still tracing your lovely profile
with warm hands, your marble bust
  incapable of outbursts or guile?

When you died, I thought the gods had
  grown even more cowardly than men;
I vowed to turn my back on them,
  to embrace only the tiny embers of joy

which illuminated your father's and
  sisters' faces, when weeks later I saw
how their eyes reflected a fierce ensnarement
  of love: your long-lashed, open-eyed measure.

In their gazes an eloquence of you still
	persisted, and this comforted me.
But, daughter, the gulfs of darkness only
	open into a more capacious darkness:

death is an emptiness spiraling into us
	like a drill, hollowing us out—deeper
and deeper—until the winds of loss
	shriek through us as through a tunnel.

Your father died. Do you know?
	Our artisans had barely finished
carving the daffodils—your favorites—
	to deck your tomb, when he, too,

succumbed to a fever, still swooning
	with grief, and wildly frantic,
knowing that death stood by his bed-
	side, an invisible sentry. He died

that same night, clutching your ribbons,
	holding my gaze tormentedly.
I lurched from him blindly—for
	I couldn't comprehend pain's roar

blasting my body, how my wracked flesh
	storehoused its tremors, its terrors,
even though my mind veered and pitched
	in a ruined stupor, numbed through

by death's narcosis, by its doubled blows.
    Silla, see how two of your sisters
stir wands of incense around your altars,
    how they cry out in their sleep, so

fearful that they'll join you and Papa,
    or that I will leave them, too.
Our days slouch and rebound from
    the tedium of our old habits.

Nothing replaces your touch or voice.
    Your father's stallions grow restless.
Who will harness them now? Who
    will tease music from his lyre?

Who will daub ointment on your wounds?
Little salamander, moss stoppers your ears.

Paula (January 382 CE)

Hieronymus and the Lion

Legends grow slowly and askant the truth:
time confounds them or entwines their heroes
like vines so that they'll bear a single flower.

The slave Androcles, spared in the arena
by the lion who remembered his kindness,
for instance, served as the hero for a story

which I witnessed first, in an earlier year,
when Hieronymus and I traveled north
from Rome to secure some sacred texts.

We traversed an open field surrounded
by forests, and paused for lunch. I watched
a caterpillar crawl comically up a stick, as

suddenly a lion burst into our midst, its
fangs bared, its tail lashing: it crouched
before us growling, sinking on its hind legs,

snarling, while we sat stupefied by fear.
Seeing we didn't move to strike him, the lion
relaxed his shoulders, lowered his large head

to lick a suppurated forepaw, his tongue
gently lapping putrid flesh, where a thorn
protruded between clenched, clotted toes.

Arced over us, a copper sky, curiously silent.
I held my breath, feeling my heart tighten
to a burl, my bowels churning, astir with bile.

My teacher stood then, speaking softly, as
he neared the beast who watched the man's
approach with veiled lids and glinting eyes.

Hieronymus crouched down slowly, and with
a mother's tenderness, plucked out the thorn,
offering it on his open palm, to calm the lion.

With bulky dignity, the creature sighed, raised
his massive muzzle and dragged his great tongue
across my mentor's grizzled head, a loud purr

rumbling the air, vibrating the ground until
a clamor of termites erupted from it, dazed
by that lush, trembling noise, that deep engine.

Nights when I'm wild with strife, when love
seems as distant as a starless abyss, when
my teacher encloses himself in a bitter solitude,

I remember that intimate kindness, his gentle
touch upon the lion's paw, how courage wells
up at unforeseen moments and blesses us all.

Paula (Rome, January 385 CE)

Obiter Dictum

He sees me merely as part of the world's calligraphy
trapped in space: I'm just an apostrophe to him,
as inconsequential as a bone discarded by a stray,
as brief and unfixed as a spasm of lightning.

All *things* are equal to him: thorn bush and wasp,
wheel spokes, braided hemp, jug and knife, the dirt.
He drags his body through his days like a sack
filled with useless organs, bothersome needs,

stale urges which he's loath to meet, being mind-
cast far from the deliberations of flesh, from self.
Years ago I starved myself for him, anointed
my limbs with mustard oil and myrrh, bathed

my words in holy water, steeped my feral desires
in lime and terror, schooled my mind in saints:
a time when I lashed myself with briars, and slept
naked in a cave, where only bats heard my prayers.

I'm an ascetic to him, not a scholar, although
I, too, plow the white fields, plant seeds, reap
a great bounty from those verses he translates.
My presence holds no volume for him, no odor,

no vibration of sound, no scale nor weight.
I'm bland as chalk, ephemeral as a dust cloud.
But my heart beats on flamboyantly: my lips
may crack and bleed, but they still sweeten air.

I'm like a sphere of amber, a life distilled
within a life: a spider caught in ambient sap.
I turn to wild nature now, a disciple of grass:
slowly I'm learning the raindrop's gospel.

Paula (Bethlehem, 392 CE)

St. Paula among the Marigolds

She's forsworn being a daughter, wife, widow, and mother;
she's savored the roles of Christ's bride, servant to the poor—
Now, within the matrix of her convent, Paula enjoys the solace
of celestial stirrings, as she moves in orbit among chaste sisters,

those numinous, meek creatures who drift along the corridors
like thistledown—whose silences signal a silken renunciation.
Their hymns' sweet notes ring in her ears, syncopating time;
so, her months and years pass, a parade of spiritual devotions.

One morning, as she weeds the convent garden, she looks up
to see a sky of *cirrus uncinus*—a backdrop of mares' tails
spun from delicate white filaments, curling into hooks, tufts—
and suddenly, mid-breath, she feels Christ's touch upon her

cheek and an abundance of grace expands her lungs until
she gasps, seeing shimmering before her a dark-eyed man
smiling down at her crouched form, his body so translucent
that the clouds radiating behind him permeate his fluid form—

He floats before her in empty air and she is poised in rapt
amazement—O stunned, O dazzled, O glorious reward—
O watcher—now look—be open-eyed—be undiminished,
for joy, joy! trumpets through her veins—blows her open—

(*Bethlehem, 399 CE*)

Deo Gratias

So many of my songs are gone from me,
and even my very voice has left me now.
—Virgil

Yearly, the slug crisscrosses his own tearstains,
the queen bee encrypts her hive with secret chambers,
the locust grafts his song upon fleeing shadows,
the worm weans herself on wolfbane, on stardust.

I sit in the heat of my own discontent, where
only the gruff sound of his voice replenishes me.
It is never enough to love, simply to love.
Better to cleave to the silver blade, its quiver.

Better to gather a basket of lilies and roses,
ivory and violet, to fast with strangers,
to bask in the body's hungers as in sunlight.
I bear witness to myself with meditation;

as one substratum of my heart calcifies,
another layer pleasures itself with memory:
my touch a chink in his armor, his touch
frugal, but scalding, and his gaze plainsong.

I grow hoarse. My virgins pile a pyramid of
fruits before me, to tempt me again to break
my fasting. I will not. Faith is episodic
initially—but these long years it's yielded

to something else . . . something slowly fluid—
a liberation of the senses, an animal wisdom.

I watch my sparrow granddaughter polish the pyx,
the nape of her neck softened by cilia of down,

her open face so like my own a lifetime ago—
contemplative as well water, a rosy cameo.
Is she suited for a nun's habit? I think perhaps
her fingers are better fitted to a cithera's strings.

Yet I find such flexibility of thought in her,
and an undefiled purity that enthralls me.
Little Paula, come sit on my wrinkled knees—
teach me to be like an angel struck dumb—

Paula (Bethlehem, Summer 403)

The Lost Diaries

Prologue

After that pious master, my father, Eusebius,
    sent me off (despite my mother's wails)
to distant Rome, I became first a scholar, then
    an orator, and, finally, a man of the world.

I lived in a dormitory for boys, all of us tutored
    by Aelius Donatus, a maestro of grammar;
I spent my adolescence studying great rhetoric
    with the eloquent harelip, Victorinus.

Hour after hour, I breathed in Virgil and Cicero,
    Sallust, Terrence, Plautus, and Horace,
or I argued over my first Greek renderings
    with my beloved, sharp-tongued Rufinus.

On Sundays my friends and I often toured
    the tombs of the apostles and martyrs.
We entered crypts dug out of earth's depths
    which, along walls on the passage's sides,

entomb the bodies of buried men and women.
    They were so dark it seemed the prophecy
of the Psalmist was fulfilled: "Let them go
    down alive into hell." Only here and there

did a ray of light penetrate from above and
    relieve the horror of the blackness.
Then we'd grope back through the darkness,
    remembering Virgil's line: "Everywhere

dread grips my heart; even the silence
frightens me." Thereafter, when I emerged
into blinding sunlight, the world appeared
irreversibly altered. Shadows deepened.

Death entered my dreams then—long weeks
I'd awaken from night terrors seizing me
by the throat, pummeling my nerves; death
lurking like a poison in my dry mouth—

So I began keeping these secret diaries, if only
to tame the demon that taunted me daily,
to know its masks, its pulse, its dark habits,
that I might banish it from my thoughts.

No one, not even Rufinus, knew of them, for
I hid my confessions under a loose stone
beneath my bed, where only occasional earwigs
danced over my sins, over my nightmares.

⁓

For sixty years I've hauled my diaries with me,
a corrupt penance, as I traversed West or East:
from Rome to Gaul and Dalmatia, then to Antioch,
where I had my fateful fever, my awful vision.

With leather thongs I strapped them to my back
before traveling across the Syrian deserts.
I took them on every pilgrimage, every journey,
finally sewing them into my undergarments.

They catalogue my most harrowing transgressions,
a purgatory of the fierce fires lit primarily by
the *flamma carnis*: my early manhood's passion
for feasting on exotic fruits, ripened flesh.

My diaries are the flint I strike my faith upon,
for how can I urge my monks away from sin,
if my own secret shame doesn't singe me?
I know my words are maggots swarming

a cesspool, and they hiss at me like serpents,
my lifelong detritus, these flakes of filth—
After I see Bethlehem one last time, and before
I meet Christ our Lord, I will burn them.

Jerome (Jerusalem, 419 CE)

St. Jerome in the Chalcis Desert

Sometimes the heart needs educating;
the bruise lightens to mauve,
and the strange alchemy

that turns charcoal and sap into
a raven, reverses itself into
a mendicant's shawl.

Though I seem a wizened presbyter,
dogma hounds me like a halo
of hookah smoke.

My knuckles grow hard as porphyry;
my monasticism enshrines me
in loss. I'm always cold,

anonymous as the quivering dormouse
who nightly revisits me, an oracle—
inside his mind's tiny orbit,

the universe whirls bravely.
Faith is a wagon drawn
by fireflies,

so there must be a going forth and
a going asunder, a blinding of
the mind's eye.

Jerome (Syria, 376 CE)

Caput Mundi

Had I a hundred tongues, a hundred lips,
a throat of iron and a chest of brass,
I could not tell men's countless sufferings.
—Virgil

Rome isn't solely the "head of the world," but also
its bowels, its biceps, stomach, its Argus-eyes.
Nightly, it sleeps among its spoils, a humped monster;
by day, Rome's an uncoiling basilisk of motion and matter.
Today, en route to the Baths of Trajan, I passed through
streets thickened by outpourings of human effluvium spewed
from the *insulae*, those island tenements of utter woe.

Such awful, howling lamentations issue from their walls!
It's as if throngs of the dying are rattling their hollow bones,
their cries amplified by a thousand bullhorns' blaring.
These alleys—peopled with lepers, amputees, the pocked
faces of smallpox victims, the deformed and hobbled,
stricken castrati who rot with gangrene, mutilated slaves—
these alleys seethe with Rome's flotsam, its shame.

I held my sleeve to my nose and mouth to block the stench
and stifle my gagging, even as I warded off pickpockets,
wounded beggars, the paraffin-thin children fated to die.
A prostitute, clearly mad, bared her scabrous breasts
to me, her nipples dribbling bloody pus, her eyes wild.
A blind woman with withered arms and tattooed cheeks
was being pumped against a wall by a brawny pygmy.

Everywhere I turned, I heard the prophet of the apocalypse
proclaiming our doom, a deep roaring in my eardrums.

I stumbled from that labyrinth, sputtering with rage,
lost in a conflagration of despair. I leaned against a pillar
and retched, then wept. I swear, Christ be my witness,
that one day I'll lead my brethren from blazing Sodom,
from this horror, this fallen world.

Jerome (Rome, 371 CE)

St. Jerome Rests from His Labors

He raises the stoneware amphora to his lips
and drinks deeply, red wine speckling his beard.

The Sabbath. A distant donkey's bray scolds him
momentarily, but he puts aside self-recriminations.

Fasting on water today isn't enough: wine rouses
his blood for the depthless hours of supplication.

Sobriety never abandons him, nor will his spine
straighten again like a sapling's: too many years

he's knelt by splay or vestibule, so many decades
of prayers, his bony knees hardened like a camel's.

On the periphery of his mind, the woman sulks.
She's done her dawn ablutions, her stint of sweeping,

making bread: she's worked silently this Sabbath,
and now she's withdrawn into a corner to mend.

Why so sullen, he asks, but Paula's lips are closed.
Sultry drafts gust around the sanctum, stirring

the dust into small piles. She begins to weep.
Were she an anvil, he would strike her hard

with the mallet of his contempt; or if she hung,
like a dull bell, he would swing her clapper

into a deafening tumult of rebuke and echo.
But she bears a mortal stench, and seems softer

than an ash with her womanly sorrow—gray,
easily rent—and he feels ambushed by pity for her,

remembering the weary leagues of their pilgrimage,
the weeks surviving on mulch, fungi, wild ginger.

He can't banish nor rid himself of her, for she
festers like a disease in his entrails, a malady

that paradoxically quickens his pulse and stops
his heart—she's his stigma, a visible reprisal

for his fiercely suppressed, dream-borne yearnings:
he knows how lust quells or dwarfs noble ambitions,

so he returns once more to his sanctum, bitter,
violently thirsty for another swig of wine.

Jerome (Bethlehem, 394 CE)

St. Jerome in Decline

Vocatus atque non vocatus deus aderit.
—Erasmus

Philo knew the primary creation to be spiritual,
the secondary creation earthly, of the body—
and I know the mind hovers between both
realms as an intermediary, an agent conveying
breath to substance, ideas to deed.

I pride myself on being a vir trilinguis,
master of three tongues, a scholar, diconate,
church Father, translator and chronicler,
historian, traveler, counselor, and theologian,
exegete and recluse, a pedagogue, librarian.

But illness breaks me and my eyesight dims
into a wintry dusk. Like the Apostle Paul,
I still retain the skill of exhortation, but
my voice erodes and my strength abates.
Always at my sleeve now: my amanuensis,

he whose baldness reveals a fontanel
beating like a newborn's, so flung into rapt
focus is he, stylus in hand, during long dictations.
My own hand turns limaceous, though my thoughts
ripple and soar as I repeat the Psalter verses.

I've grown old. My thoughts ramble.
To us men, this life is a racecourse:
we contend here, we are crowned elsewhere.

No man can lay aside fear while serpents
beset his path. I dread impurity, but find

even in my decline, the footprints
of the devil lead my thoughts: *his strength*
is in the loins, and his force is in the navel—
thus must I make my final passage by
relinquishing all fleshly enticements.

These diaries record unholy ruminations—
my fatal circles of affection—but they capture
only half the man, a fresco barely penciled in:
the incomplete phantom of my contraband self,
a counter-life—intimate, dangerous as Pandora's box.

One by one, my friends have been taken from me,
my correspondents fade, then disappear into
death's grotto, and only the gentle attentions of
Melania and the younger Paula bestir me with hope.
I am overburdened, still, by the sack of Rome,

by the putrid rise of Pelagianism, by the death
of my old debater and rival, dear, feeble Rufinus.
All Christendom seems under siege as hordes
of barbarians sweep across the Empire, the streets
crowded with battered fugitives, starving refugees.

Deprivations, burning monasteries in Bethlehem,
my estrangement from Jerusalem's Bishop—
censure and petty arguments, hindrances, panics,
derision from my clerical foes, laughable contempt.
And Paula's absence most diminishes me.

Jerome (Bethlehem, 399 CE)

St. Jerome Alone

He wanders the graveyard stricken with loss.
The candelabrum he carries trails hot wax across

the flagstone steps he treads, burns his knuckles:
but he's oblivious, as usual, to pain's stratagems.

He hopes to find communion here, at her crypt,
to enrich his anguish, or assuage it, by straining

toward a strangeness which consumes him now
in her absence, steeping his life in bewilderment.

He was stupid with love for her, soiled and pricked
by unspoken affection, halved and quartered by her—

stung, flailed, roused, entangled, assailed over
and over again by her erudition, her stately grace,

by her silent forbearance, her womanly cheer,
by her softness—as if, particle by minute particle,

she arose from an embankment of clouds—and
by her devotion, so pure it rivaled the Virgin's.

Her grave is strewn with fresh laurel leaves,
with the detritus from straw wreaths, wild roses,

willow strands that scampering insects plunder.
He sets down the flickering candles to crouch

beside the planed surfaces of smooth marble,
to press his forehead against the cold tomb.

She was nothing and everything to him:
ardent follower, servant and sister, gleaner

of verses, a progenitor of propriety, noun
wed to his verbs, a grain of salt, speckle of

dew on the green blade of each rising day,
ghost, caulk of his lonely hours, companion.

She moved so gently through his world that
molecules of air were barely stirred to step

aside, and rivulets of wind dispersed to spend
their vanishing in a quiet abstraction of sighs.

He recalls her luminous, dreamy face, her
life forever hovering between two realms—

and he feels the stale air stir and quicken
with her mild electricity, as if she's begun

to occupy his flesh invisibly, as if her body
whirls on within him, as his own destiny.

Jerome (Bethlehem, January 30, 404 CE)

A Letter from the Abbess Paula the Younger

The days of man are but as grass; for he flourisheth as a flower of the field. For as soon as the wind goeth over it, it is gone: and the place thereof shall know it no more.
—Psalm 103:15

Dearest Cousin,
I have found among our deceased spiritual grandfather's effects
several codices bound in twine and goat leather,
and greatly damaged by the hungry meanderings of white ants,
by inclement storage, and—I suspect—by secreted tears.

I am shocked by the stark revelations
from these tawdry looking, embattled, filth-covered, embittered diaries.
Apostasy threatens their author; a barbarism of the mind
overcomes his wisdom, and a crucified spirit's tortured ravings
infiltrate their pages.

We thought we knew the man: we did not.
Could not have. So much within our hearts howls for forgiveness,
withers us, while Lucifer stands ever ready to entice us,
to harvest our sins. Jerome's private pen stuttered and
raged self-calumny, even as his public letters proved him righteous.

There is too much mystery in man,
as in the Eternal. Too great a hydra, this person to whom
our grandmother wed her life and her soul. In them both, earthly love—
that euphoria, that dread which ravishes—vied with divine love.
I grew up in the humid greenhouse of their devotion.

What to do with these diaries?
I believe their famed author would have me burn them.
Indeed, I've taken the liberty of destroying three pages which

alluded to our Elder Paula serving as an *agapeta* to Jerome—yes,
believe it!—as his priestly mistress!

I also put to flame several salacious pages
recounting how he lay with two licentious nuns—a triangulation
of orgiastic fumblings worthy (you'd remind me) of those oversexed tales
of Bacchus and of Sappho's sultry lovers on Lesbos—
Scandalous such outpourings. His fantasies saddened me.

So the scales have fallen from my unworldly eyes.
I see now, Cousin, how futilely we strive against our natures:
we desire what is alien to us, otherworldly, other than ourselves—
and such yearning tonsures our souls' wings. God lurks
behind and beyond our mirrors—

We struggle like flies to escape this vortex of sins.
We live in exile from our physical bodies.
Slumbering bears, we hibernate inside our deaths,
dreamless, waiting to be reborn again.
We stand facing God, our mouths agape.

Assyrian, African, Jew and Egyptian, even the loin-
clothed Brahman and chanting Buddhist of whom Jerome spoke
in his letters—anchorite or centurion, Essene or harlot—what we want,
both in the kingdom of man and in the promise of heaven, is *transcendence*,
a harmony of breath with the divine—

A rebel angel he was, Cousin.
Bless Jerome's bones. Bless Paula's long-dried tears.
Herein I enclose the remainder of his writings.

Your faithful servant and friend,
chaste bride of Christ,
Paula.

Paula the Younger (Bethlehem, c. 440 CE)

New Poems

(2010–2016)

Alone

I like my solitude,
This cowl I've borne
Upon my back—since torn
From amniotic sac—and which
I'll wear into decrepitude.
It is a veil both thin and rich,
This shroud that's spirit-toothed,
This briefly castled interlude.

River Lamps

At which temple should she worship? An imprint of a thumb was enfleshed in her palm, a sign that bespoke (according to India's most famed palmist) her otherworldly, sacred powers. Could she, like Siddhartha, abandon her past and embark on a self-exiled journey toward enlightenment? She was twenty and jangling with music when she walked, her silver anklets and bracelets beguiling the air. She wore the invisible chains of desire draped around her neck, her nipples, navel, and loins.

All life in Chennai bore a golden glare: the city shimmered and burned. One night, during Diwali, she walked across the Cooum River Bridge to gaze down at a thousand tiny oil lamps riding the darkened sludge like fiery eyes. Sweat bloomed on her brow. She saw the charred bodies of the dead as swaddled barges, their bones turning to gypsum, their skulls (once the humming beehives of her daydreams), now swarming with maggots. She shuddered in her mortal shroud, poised at the world's edge, and entered a region of sorrow from which there is no return.

The Women of Juárez

There are bones strewn in arroyos and fields here that weep in their marrow.
Bones of little girls, their skulls and femurs; bones of teenagers, small ribcages
and delicate metatarsals; bones of young women, pelvises and spinal columns.
Twenty years of bones scattered like casual debris from over six hundred girls—
their laughter and giggles broken from their mouths, their tears burning the
dry soil like acid. Even the desert sparrows sit dazed on their branches; even the
lizards shrink from their own shadows. In houses all over Ciudad Juárez, mothers
and fathers sit stupefied by their windows. Their hands tremble as they reach out
to open their doors, when they touch their daughters, their breathing daughters.
What has happened to the beautiful girls of Juárez—the ones who blushed at
their quinceañeras, who walked dry fields at dusk, never returning from work
at the factories? Who raped and tortured them, burned and disposed of them?
What kind of men are these, what kind of men, I ask you, who have black bile in
their veins, whose minds overflow with toxins, whose hearts are concrete—and
why, oh why has no one stopped them?

The Prisoner

It didn't matter that she'd taken a self-defense class
the previous summer, nor that she was good and brave:

a man broke into her apartment, held her at knifepoint
for over five hours, and did terrible things to her.

She didn't know then, being eighteen and naïve,
and too ashamed to tell anyone about her ordeal,

why she'd had to stand in the shower afterwards
for an hour, nor why she couldn't sleep for months,

even with every light turned on in her sister's house,
nor why she couldn't bear to look in black men's faces,

too terrified to share the same sidewalk with them.
Only years later did she learn there was a name for it:

post-traumatic stress disorder, but it did no good.
Something inside of her had grown twisted

into barbed wire, and when
she walked, it cut her.

This Lion

I wish he would stalk into my bedroom
this wintry moonlit night—unstealthily—
his mane tinged with a platinum sheen.
Then he'd creak open his cavernous mouth

and emit a rumbling mechanical roar—
Perhaps there'd be a clicking sound
as he flutters his horsehair eyelashes,
and a dim whirring from his heart's gears

as they spin and turn like the giant wheels
in a colossal clock made for an empress.
I have dreamed his entry into my house,
into my mind, so many times that I can smell

his grassy breath—no gazelle eater he—
and gaze deeply into his saucer-sized eyes,
brown as the muddy Zambezi River's shore.
He's the totem and vehicle I've called forth

to vanquish the new terrors in my life:
my dying mother's unspeakable suffering,
her mortality that is my own, my gown;
my father's mindlessness, his absence,

the black hole of his memory into which
I fall endlessly; my soul corroding pain
mimicking Edvard Munch's silent howl—
Come in, tin lion! Devour these calamities,

until you're as sated as after a zebra feast.
I'm alone—as always—with my despair,
and it will swallow me alive, unless you
get here fast, oh my dear mechanical beast—

Egypt Liberated

Libya in turmoil, the dictator
ordering his troops to murder
protestors rallying in the streets.
UN plans a "no fly" zone there.

Our local mayor and his cronies
indicted for corruption.
FOX News blames teachers
for the crashing economy.

But more dire and more urgent:
my mother, a vessel of goodness—
brimming with sweetness and love—
struggles heroically to stay alive.

Her body overtaken by anarchy:
unwholesome cells on the rampage,
marauders attacking lungs and brain.
Radiation ignites her gray matter.

Chemo muddles her mind further,
and she downs a battery of drugs
until her mind blurs, her hands shake,
she cannot walk, she weeps in pain.

I don't care about the world's woes,
about tyranny in the Middle East—
for my beloved mother is the world to me,
and, like Egypt, she deserves to be free.

(Arab Spring, 2011)

I Won't Pretend

anymore that you're immortal,
for now the clock's ticking madly
as your renegade squamous cells
multiply like a nasty rumor gone
haywire in the township of your body.
Your chest hurts, and your voice
is hoarse some days, and you're
so weak, Mother, you can barely
talk on the phone when I call—
Oh, where's the town crier who
would call the Guard to arms?
Where's the Mayor with his
preparations to fortify the body
politic within a fortress, to shield
you from enemies both without
and within? And where is your
genius loci—clasping a cup of wine,
a cornucopia of magic serums,
and his rat-catching serpent—
that He-spirit who should be hurling
your disease into oblivion?
Your heart bravely patters on.
Surely it's aglow, casting its rays
over friend and foe alike, brilliant
and mysterious as tonight's full moon,
which brims with mortal light.

If I Could

I'd hold your lifeless hand, Mother,
for as long as it might take to bring an ignition
of life back to it, to you and your girlish body.

Eighty-five and your legs seemed as lithe
as a dancer's, your waist still the envy of
many a young woman's, and your smile—

it was truly dazzling, contagious, luminous as
a sadhu's or newborn babe's, as a visionary's.
So, as you lay dying on your hospital bed,

I thought you'd become like Dorian Gray—
some long ago, hidden self-portrait aging while
you grew younger and younger. Your face

shed its wrinkles, your skin turned smooth as
satin, your eyes shone with childlike glee,
and your baby-fine hair sprouted in tiny wisps.

But you were growing backward into your death,
turning away from the world of mumbling beings,
away from the filigree of invisible threads binding

you to us, us to you—from our not wanting you
ever to disappear from our touch, from our gazes.
I held your hand, saw your fingernails turn blue,

and I knew then you were already beyond
all our saving, beyond hope of returning.

Baila-Ma

It happened like lightning, with abrupt power.
It occurred as in a nightmare, with the windows
flung open and the air howling through them:
it was a crushing torrent, with its tsunami
of grief and endless wailing.

You were so ill, Mother, and the days flew by
without mercy, and all your dazzling gifts faded,
one by one, and your generous voice
was forever silenced.

My house is aglow with your paintings
from Europe and Hermosa Beach:
canvases, like descendants, scores of them,
alive and still, still alive.

How I miss your laugh, your terrible jokes
that made us groan in unison like schoolgirls.
I miss your touch, your broad maternal gaze
that took in all of me, nerves and fibers, dark heart
and queasy soul. I even miss your quick-fire anger.

In the quietest hours I long for you, when
your vacancy empties out the world.

The look of utter surprise on your face
when you died.

Death simplifies a life until it's only
a silhouette, then a vague outline,
then merely ellipses . . .

After that last agonizing breath, we women—
two daughters and your saintly nurse, Pearla—
encircled your delicate body, a chrysalis,
to preserve and memorize your gaunt beauty.

Knowing they would embarrass you
even in death, I plucked two silver hairs
from your chin, before the rabbi walked in
to take your body away from us.

Gone

Where do they go, the dead,
without their jumpsuits of flesh
and their servile shadows?

Do they rise to the ceiling,
as returnees have avowed,
to stare down at flaccid bodies,

awed by their immobility and
pallor, only to rise even farther,
erupting through high ceilings

into the vapors of midnight,
slipping away into the ether
of the far stratospheres?

And is there a gathering place
for the souls of the dead,
a place in the Beyond,

that dimension known by physicists,
where spirits reform their energy
and prepare to be reborn into

a new life, be it human or not?
I'd like to *know* where you've gone,
Mother, so I may turn my gaze

and yearning toward your light,
in whatever form it has taken—
and nestle again in my self.

Mother My Ship

Mother my ship,
my course, my sound,
what will I do
now you have drowned?

Where will I sleep,
how will I steer,
where will I go?

O where can I sail
without your compass,
your vim and valor?

How will I know
in torrents ahead
lie danger or rainbow,
when Mother my good
bright love is dead—

How does it feel
to dwell in the sky
without mast or galley
and sun for an eye?

With cloud your shroud,
who mothers me now?

(after May Swenson)

Martin Falk's Last Photographs

I took your digital camera's memory card to Target yesterday—two years after your death—to print your final pictures. There are fourteen of them, all taken (I'm guessing) a few weeks before you left our world: four close-up photos of lavish magenta azaleas and petticoat-pink roses, a reminder of the world's robust beauty, then two images of your beloved Margit's bronze grave marker and her smaller memorial tablet in the synagogue at the City of Hope Hospital. There are three other pictures of the cemetery where you're both now buried: one image is of a line of tall Italian cypresses that form a barrier between the cemetery and the run-down apartments next door. Their elongated conical shadows cast a semi-circle of enormous fangs that stretch out in a yawn across the grass near your grave markers.

There's another (incongruous, surprising) photo of two healthy chickens—a Rhode Island Red and a chocolate brown pullet—scrambling out of some bushes adjacent to the graveyard's cypress trees. When you shot them, you must have momentarily relished the comical absurdity of those escaped birds running around that somber place. The third and last cemetery photo is of you, dear father-in-law, staring into the camera as you hold it up before your unshaven, haggard face. There's an open, vulnerable, raw grief in your eyes and slack mouth. Your skin looks washed out, newsprint gray. You look bewildered, lost. This photo breaks my heart.

You took the last five photos in your assisted living apartment. Two pictures document your living-room treasures: your '50s walnut credenza containing tchotchkes from Holland, Java, and Israel; your antique sword and dagger collection hung above it on the wall, surrounding your Viennese father's round Turkish carpet; a lovely, faux marble Aphrodite torso; and a framed, color photograph of you and Margit, taken during the prime of your lives. You look tanned and happy, with the tragedies of the War only a distant echo buried deep within your rib cages—

The third and last living-room photo is a still life of your many canes and walking sticks petaling out of their metal container. I can't help but puzzle over why you documented them. Did you want to remind us how difficult walking had become for you, those last months of your life? Or, were you worried one of the house-keeping crew might steal one? Or, perhaps you thought the image was idiosyncratically compelling, artsy, somehow? Maybe you were saying good-bye to those canes, since you'd no longer need them in the beyond.

You snapped the last two pictures while lying in bed in your bedroom. I recognize the old wood headboard behind you, and the Dhuri rug hung above it. As with your self-portrait in the cemetery, these two photographs deliberately expose your grief, your unshuttered despair. It's as if you're looking death in the face, even while leaving us yet another encoded (and baffling) visual postcard. Martin, there's such a wildness in your eyes, and such loneliness. Why did you want us to see your suffering in this exposed and vulnerable way? Did we ever really know you?

(November 1, 2013)

The Inheritance

That she should *not* be here—
feet infirmly planted on a stoop or stair—
this vanishing she could not abide:
this loosening slide from her mortal skin,
this obvious lie.
No, eighty-five and still stunning
with her platinum hair, slender shadow,
her persistent desire;

she would trick death, don a camouflage
(whooping crane? candlestick? Cymbidium?),
or will herself into a dormant
transparency—She'd huddle into
a quivering single cell of eternal life—
Oh, endless, endless, endless—
and *here* she is
tearing my eyelid.

Dear Old Dad

When I see you slumped in a chair
at our raucous family gatherings,
your blue eyes glazed, your frail body
curled in on itself, I still see, Father,
the ghost of your younger selves:
the dashing, secretive philanderer speeding
through Hermosa Beach in your "green hornet"
or red Alfa Romeo to the hills of Palos Verdes,
a look of wild glee on your handsome face—
or the composer perched in an easy chair, clad only
in boxers, while conducting a Mahler symphony.

You seem only semi-conscious now,
lost in some ongoing dream, yet your eyes
don't change: they're clear as the Adriatic,
on whose shores we camped like gypsies
over a half century ago, in the summer of '56.
I was five then, a scrawny kid and shy like you.
Mom and you sunbathed, smoked debonairly,
spoke Italian with locals. At dusk you built me
exquisite sand castles: intricately decked
with scores of spires, flotsam ramps, moats,
tiered towers, canals, and drawbridges.
When the tide devoured your masterpieces,
I was horrified. You simply laughed.

Dear Father, you're more of a mystery
to me now than ever. I don't know how
to reach you, your mind's so distant
from mine, and it travels silently.
You speak rarely. When I see you,

I see a ghost, for I'm the haunted one,
I'm the one who's lost.

The Father of All Things

When we found you yesterday, after our walk,
abloom with bruises, bloodied, ashen-faced,
in shock after having fallen twice on the floor
and then struggling to remember how to rise,

I knew, Dad, desperation and fear roused you
to your knees, to your trembling feet again.
How to go on living in limbo, with all systems
failing, and as the world grows more remote?

You've been the father of all things for us,
your unwise daughters. Now we lay helpless
before time's crushing wheels to which we, too,
are pinned like damaged butterflies. I'd believe

in *samādhi*, if I could, that death will liberate you,
return your soul to some great iCloud in eternity—
you who's frail as an ancient scroll. Your faint voice,
pale ink from bleached sea grass, grows translucent.

Can I believe you'll be freed from your body's bondage,
set adrift in the cosmos like a pigeon's under-feather?
Everything you've been and will be lies emblazoned
in your damaged brain, photos yet undeveloped.

Elegy at Midnight

Gone, gone, forever gone,
Father, left, lost, leaving behind
only grief and a thin rain falling outside.

Gone into ash soon, Father, then
into the gloom of a dark mausoleum
where only the ghosts of fossilized beings

inhabit its cold, marbleized silence,
where your blurred spirit will be stayed—
unless our love can set it free again.

Gone, gone my childhood furies,
my adoration, too—oh Father come back
like a wound reopened, unsealed,

your blood racing back into our veins,
your voice deep and plaintive in our ears,
your heart thumping its music wildly again.

Return to us even as you were: barely
half alive, drooping like a spent day lily,
that we may hold you to us once more,

forever, if only we could, if only—
if flesh could rise again from the void,
if our gasps could reawaken your breath—

if you would not leave us so alone,
if only you'd stayed—oh stay a while longer,
and we'll never again loosen our grasp—

(January 26, 2013)

The Consolations of Love

When we float on our backs down-river,
the sky becomes a runway for taxiing clouds;
wild geese paddle above us like novitiates.

For the ancient and immoveable boulder,
a solitary eucalyptus sheds its bark
in a slow-motion strip tease. Nearby,
two grosbeaks groom each other's mites.

Who are the mysterious heirs to night,
but the slack-mouthed roses fading in dark,
and the rustproof stars sharpening their kisses?

When he skims across the glassy surface,
the water strider believes he is a god,
until he feels a tug in his pulse
that isn't hunger.

At dawn the young husband quietly rises
and glances down at his placid wife,
her lashes black as tar-dipped feathers.

Not happiness, just a salty peace—
sitting in sagging beach chairs,
the long-wedded couple stares off
in different directions, north and south.

Dog Sleeping

Those strange voices the dog hears
in her sleep: wolves howling with a rising moon,
perhaps, or the rush of froth over black pebbles
in an icy stream? She twitches in her dreamscape,
her tongue lopsidedly dangling from her black lips.

What atavistic fears fuel her hyper-panting now,
forepaws scrambling in a pantomime gallop,
clacking sideways against the wood floorboards?
Reindeer stampeding, or merely her nightmare
of being chased by a gang of hirsute suitors?

Wake up, Lily. There are tabbies to stare down,
and a kid carrying a surfboard up the street—
two visions that raise a Mohawk along your spine.
But look! She's leapt to her feet and raced out,
lickity split, to our open balcony to bark

at a proper threat: a noisy family who's carrying
beach towels, umbrella, a huge bag of chips.
Silly dog. Or I suspect she's getting cataracts,
just like me—or she's caught a whiff of something
dangerous, a disease? Dogs can sniff cancer,

it's said, just as they can read people's faces.
Back asleep, Lily snores softly, dreaming again,
ears perked up pointedly, eyelids squinching;
her nostrils open to inhale ten thousand scents,
as the world spins on atop its tipped axis.

(San Clemente, California)

Late November Lament

Does our six-foot bear mind getting drenched?
This is what I ask at midnight, my head throbbing,
rain flinging its tirade aslant against the panes.
Since Halloween he's camped under the pond deck
like some wayward deity, coming out to plop heavily
into the cold, black waters, then standing shoulder-deep
and swiveling his neck to catch the flash of trout
we've raised from fingerlings—raised not to eat
but to rob the summer mosquitoes of our flesh.
It's pouring down sheets now, but I can hear him
lumbering across the planks—it's not thunder—
the yellow map of India on his chest probably
shining its strange beacon, and isn't he a lord of
some sort? Isn't he the wilderness we came to desire,
though not in XXL, not so roughshod and sour-
faced, not reeking of musk and garbage and brute force?
Something about him makes me sad and happy,
as if his mortal stench could pluck me out of myself
and transform me into a goddess of prophecies.
But that's just my painkillers talking, as the rain
pummels this hungry bear eschewing sleep,
who blinks away streamers of water as he turns
his slurred gaze to my lit window, as he issues
his sodden grunts into the patter, and later loosens
a pyramid of steaming shit next to my poet's bench.

Dawn over the Tiber River

A hundred thousand starlings rise
skyward in fluid streams and swelling throngs,

spinning, looping, stretching their chirping flocks like taffy
above the platinum, shimmering water,

their ten-ten thousand cries like stampeding waterfalls,
or electronic music gone viral in the chilled air.

A five-mile-long serpentine river of dark, speckled birds
is rushing headlong into a new day

at the end of a terrible year, a year full of terrors:
death of thousands from the Fukushima tsunami,

oh death of my beautiful, delicate mother,
and death of my husband's lonely, soldiering father.

But the day is born anew, the starlings singing and
winging their terrifying joy into a world

that's fresh with dew on the surface of cars, bridges,
and ancient Roman ruins. Only look!

There's the fallen Emperor Nero, crowned
with a dripping ring of bird guano.

Simply to be born is enough sometimes,
much harder to endure.

(Rome, November 2011)

Notes and Dedications

I've arranged this collection's volumes chronologically, from my oldest to my most recently published books. (Although *Cartographies* was published in 2008, most of the book's poems were composed between 1980 and 2000.)

Questions My Daughters Asked Me, Answers I Never Gave Them:

This seven-part poem was published in 1999 by *Solo* magazine, and reprinted with my permission as a beautiful limited-edition chapbook by Jean Gillingwators and Anna Alquitela at Blackbird Press in 2014.

Poems from *The Enchanted Room* (1986):

"Tat Tvam Asi"—*Tat tvam asi* is from the Sanskrit and means "that thou art." *Kaṭṭumarām* is the Tamil word and origin of the English "catamaran" (a kind of sailboat). The phrase *Tat tvam asi* is drawn from the ancient Chandogya Upanishad. Each section of this chapter closes with a father instructing his son: "Sarvam tat satyam sa atma *tat tvam asi* Svetaketu iti." ("All is that truth. He is the soul, *that thou art*, oh Svetaketu.") I'm indebted to Robert Falk for his translation.

"The Bearer's Son"—In an Indian household a bearer serves the same function as a butler.

Copious thanks to Sam Hamill and Tree Swenson for publishing my first two volumes of poetry with Copper Canyon Press, thus launching my public life in letters.

Poems from *Days of Awe* (1989):

Poet William Matthews selected "Survival" for the $500 SCCE International Poetry Prize in 1984.

"King Midas's Daughter"—This poem is dedicated to my late and dearest father, a bon vivant, composer, and ethnomusicologist, Robert Leopold Simon (1923–2013).

I'm deeply grateful to my radiant mother, Los Angeles artist Baila Goldenthal (1925–2011), whose brilliant paintings adorn the covers of *The Days of Awe*, *The Enchanted Room*, and this volume, and which inspired and illuminate the WEAVERS poems.

Poems from *Speaking in Tongues* (1990):

The other epigraph that precedes "Origins" is from T. S. Eliot's poem "Little Gidding," and it reads as follows: "We shall not cease from exploration, / And the end of all our exploring / Will be to arrive where we started / And know the place for the first time."

My humblest thanks to former editor Peter Stitt, who took an enormous risk by publishing the entire "Origins" poem in the premier issue of the *Gettysburg Review*, long before it appeared in this volume.

Poems from *The Golden Labyrinth* (1995):

Generous thanks to the Fulbright Foundation for awarding me a 1990–1991 Fellowship to live for six months in Bangalore, South India, for the sole purpose of composing this book.

"Want"—Holy men and women in India usually spend their later years as wandering mendicants whose sole possessions are a begging bowl, a walking stick, and the clothes they wear upon their backs.

"Dharma"—*Salaam alekum, alekum salaam* is a common Urdu greeting and response.

"Alex in Hindustan"—*Sadhus* are Hindu holy men and women. This poem, and "Elegy in a Snow-storm," are dedicated to my beloved friend, writer Alex Londres (1950–1988), who died from AIDS, and who was portrayed by actor Antonio Banderas in the film *Philadelphia*.

"Bangalore Lullaby"—*Ratri-rani* is the fragrant "queen of the night" jasmine that is pervasive in South India.

Poems from *A Brief History of Punctuation* (2002):

Many thanks to Stephen Corey for publishing this work in the University of Georgia Press and the *Georgia Review's* illustrious 2000 chapbook series. I'm also deeply grateful to writers and publishers Chad and Beth Oness for publishing their remarkable and resplendent letterpress edition of this book.

Poems from *Ghost Orchid* (2004):

The "ghost orchid" (*dendrophylax lindenii*) "is a beautiful and curiously leafless epiphyte that lives in Fakahatchee Strand and a few other swamps in south Florida. Donovan Correll (1950), a noted orchid biologist, described the flower as a 'snow-white frog suspended in midair.'" From *Swamp Song*, by Ron Larson (University Press of Florida, 1995), p. 66.

"Benediction" is influenced by and dedicated to Allen Ginsberg, in memoriam, April 5, 1997.

Deepest thanks to Kate Gale and Mark Cull, editor and publisher of Red Hen Press, for publishing *Ghost Orchid* and *Cartographies*.

Poems from *WEAVERS* (2005):

These ekphrastic poems were inspired by an eponymous series of two-dozen paintings of weavers by Los Angeles artist, and my beloved mother, Baila Goldenthal. Fine letterpress publisher Jean Gillingwators, founder and editor of Blackbird Press, and her assistant, Anna Aquitela, published the reproductions of Goldenthal's WEAVERS paintings opposite these ekphrastic poems in her gorgeous 2005 edition of this book.

Weavers Series (1989–1994): The artist uses the "Old Master" technique of oil glazing over tempera on wood panels. The Gothic and Romanesque shapes of some of the panels, the use of shallow space, the stylization of the figures, are art history references. All contribute to a wedding of technique and concept as they combine with the enigmatic [and often androgynous] figures and the metaphorical use of the weaver's loom. As that series developed, the hands became more and more important, and seemed to demand a separate, and more direct exploitation of the original concept. Thus evolved the paintings that became the *Cat's Cradle Series*. (This commentary is by Baila Goldenthal.)

Poems from *Cartographies* (2008):

"Snow" is dedicated to my mother-in-law, Margit Idelovici Falk. She was born in Vienna, Austria on November 1, 1921, and died on September 15, 2007. During World War II, the Japanese military imprisoned her for more than three years in Java, where she'd fled in 1939 to live with Dutch relatives. All but one of Margit's family members died in Europe, victims of the Nazis; her younger brother, Walter Idelovici, walked overland from Austria to Palestine, and died in Israel's first battle for independence in 1949. The loose translation for the German phrase "Du bist verrückt!" is "You're crazy!"

"Second Born" is for my younger daughter, Leah Falk.

"Dulce et Decorum Est" is for Jack Miles, visionary mentor, profound thinker, and critical guide.

"Bark with Authority" is for my dear friend, Cynthia Tuell, and her faithful dogs, Molly and Mercy, my hiking partners for many intrepid years.

"El Día de los Muertos" is dedicated to my formidably talented former student, the poet and playwright, Diana Marie Delgado.

"City of Angels" is also dedicated to my daughter, Leah Falk. This poem and "Dulce et Decorum Est" refer to the riots in Los Angeles in April 1992, following the acquittal of the police officers who brutally beat LA resident Rodney King.

"Waste Management" is for my neighbor and friend of many years, Patricia Chapman, and for Gerard and Noelle Morrison, ambivalent fans of the TV series, *The Sopranos*.

"Marriage Vow" is for my husband, Robert Falk.

"Black Widow" is dedicated to my former colleague, the brilliant writer Chris Abani.

"The Voyage" is for Grace and Barry Sanders, with abundant love.

Poems from *The Raindrop's Gospel* (2010):

These poems are drawn imaginatively from the *Letters* of St. Jerome. I have interspersed within Jerome and Paula's stories direct quotations drawn from his voluminous *Letters*. I have italicized those lines and passages that contain verbatim excerpts from his *Letters*. My primary source for the English translations of Jerome's *Letters* was *A Select Library of Nicene and Post-Nicene Fathers of the Christian Church, Second Series, Volume VI: St. Jerome: Letters and Select Works*, translated by W. H. Fremantle, G. Lewis, and W. G. Martley (James Parker & Co., Oxford, 1893). During the earlier periods of his life, and before his ordination as a priest, Jerome was known as "Hieronymus."

"Father of Punctuation"—St. Jerome purportedly earned this title (long after his death) for his attempts to standardize the use of punctuation marks in sacred texts.

"A Matriarch of Rome"—*Dum spiro spero*: "As long as I breathe, I hope." My sincere thanks to John Felstiner from Stanford University for bringing this anonymous quotation to my attention.

"Obiter Dictum"—The poem's title, from the Latin, means "an aside."

"St. Paula among the Marigolds"—The ecstatic lines in this poem's last stanza were influenced by a poem entitled "The Classic" by Polish poet Wisława Szymborska.

From "The Lost Diaries"—*In girum imus nocte et consumimur igni*: "In circles we go in the night and are consumed by fire." I'm indebted to French composer, Philippe Bodin, for teaching me this fine aphoristic Latin palindrome. The following "Rome" poem is drawn from Jerome's fictitious "Lost Diaries," as are additional poems whose lines are centered typographically.

"Rome" (361 CE)—Since and beyond their youth, Rufinus was Jerome's dearest friend; in later years he became one of Jerome's foremost theological foes.

"Caput Mundi"—The epigraph from Virgil appears in *Letter LX*, paragraph 16.

"St. Jerome Alone"—*Letter CVIII*, one of Jerome's longest letters, seeks to console Eustochium on the recent loss of her mother. The letter includes this inscription Jerome wrote and had cut on Paula's tomb: "Within this tomb a child of Scipio lies, / A daughter of the far-famed Pauline house, /

A scion of the Gracchi, of the stock / Of Agamemnon's self, illustrious: / Here rests the lady Paula, well-beloved / Of both her parents, with Eustochium / For daughter; she the first of Roman dames / Who hardship chose and Bethlehem for Christ."

"A Letter from the Abbess Paula the Younger"—By the second and third centuries CE the codex—a collection of papyrus sheets fastened by a spine and bound in protective covers—had become the common book form for Greek literature and the Christian Bible. Jewish scriptures were still inscribed and preserved on rolled papyrus or parchment scrolls. (Colin H. Roberts and T. C. Skeat, *The Birth of the Codex*, Oxford University Press, London, 1983). *Agapetae* (from the Greek: "beloved ones") were women who lived with unmarried clergy as spiritual sisters, but who sometimes also served them as mistresses. Jerome mentions them in *Letter XXII*, paragraph 14.

Bountiful thanks to Dana Curtis, editor and publisher *par excellence* of Elixir Press, who selected this book for Elixir Press's 2009 prize, and who published this novel-in-verse, *The Raindrop's Gospel*, in 2010.

New Poems (2010–2016):

Many of the poems in this section are elegies, since both my parents and my in-laws died within a short period of time, ushering in a long period of mourning.

"Alone" appeared in the *New Yorker* (September 6, 1999).

"River Lamps" appeared in the twenty-fifth anniversary anthology issue of *Kestrel* magazine, edited by John Hoppenthaler.

"The Inheritance" is dedicated to my late mother-in-law, Margit Falk.

"The Father of All Things" is for my sister, Tamara Ambroson.

"Elegy at Midnight" is for Marilyn Micheau.

"Late November Lament" is for my brilliant pain management physician, Dr. Eric Cheeho Kim.

"Dawn over the Tiber River" was included in a collaborative (ekphrastic) art exhibition, entitled *Convergence: The Poetic Dialogue Project*. The poem appeared alongside the visual art of Donna June Katz, and it was mounted at the Ukrainian Institute of Modern Art in Chicago in February and March of 2015. Artist and activist, Beth Shadur, curated the exhibit. The Chaparral Canyon Press included "Dawn over the Tiber River" in their poetry anthology, *Open Doors: An Invitation to Poetry* (Yorba Linda, CA, 2016). Many thanks to poet and editor Jie Tian and her co-editors, Irena Praitis and Natalie Graham.

Biographical Note

Maurya Simon is the author of nine acclaimed volumes of poetry. Simon's poems have appeared in over two hundred literary magazines, and she's published her work in scores of distinguished anthologies across the country. She has received numerous national awards, including an Indo/American Fulbright Fellowship (for a six-month-long residency in Bangalore, South India), a National Endowment for the Arts Fellowship in Poetry, and two distinguished prizes from the Poetry Society of America. Simon has also twice served as a Visiting Artist at the American Academy in Rome. She has given poetry readings throughout the US and in Europe and India. Maurya Simon taught college-level literature and creative writing for thirty years, and she is currently a Professor Emerita in Creative Writing and a Professor of the Graduate Division at the University of California, Riverside. She lives with her husband in the Angeles National Forest in the San Gabriel Mountains.